THE HISTORIES

By
Herodotus Halicarnassus

Abridged from George Rawlinson
by Stamati Crook

Copyright Stamati Crook © 2022

All rights reserved. Neither this book nor any portion thereof may be reproduced or used in any manner whatsoever without the express written permission of the publisher, with the exception of the use of brief quotations in a book review or scholarly journal.

First Printing: 2022

ISBN 978-0-9556859-4-1

Redware Research Limited
32 Welbeck Avenue
Hove
BN3 4JL
ENGLAND.

Web: www.concise.press
Email: sales@concise.press

Special discounts are available on quantity purchases by corporations, associations, educators and others. For details, contact the publisher at the above address.

Cover photograph of Darius the Great by Peter.ZN1 taken from Wikipedia -Attribution-ShareAlike 4.0 International (CC BY-SA 4.0).

Translation by George Rawlinson from 1858 of The Histories by Herodotus is in the public domain.

Thank you to Peter McKeever for proof-reading services

Γιά τη μάννα μου γιατί μία μάννα έχουμε.

CONTENTS

- **THE HISTORIES** I
- **CONTENTS** I
- **INTRODUCTION** 1
- **LYDIA** 4
  - GYGES 4
  - ARION 6
- **CROESUS** 8
  - ATYS 10
  - PROPHECY 11
  - PISISTRATUS 12
  - LACEDAEMONIANS 14
  - LYDIANS AND MEDES 15
  - CAPPADOCIA 16
  - THYREA 17
  - SIEGE OF SARDIS 18
  - LYDIA 21
- **CYRUS THE GREAT** 22
  - CYAXARES 23
  - ASTYAGES 24
  - PERSIA REVOLTS 26
  - PERSIANS 28
  - IONIANS 30
  - BABYLON 32
  - BABYLONIANS 35
  - QUEEN TOMYRIS 36
- **EGYPT** 40

- NILE 41
- **CAMBYSES** **46**
  - CONQUEST OF EGYPT 46
  - MEMPHIS 48
  - PSAMMENITUS 49
  - ETHIOPIA..50
  - APIS..51
  - POLYCRATES 54
- **DARIUS**... **57**
  - SMERDIS THE IMPOSTER..58
  - SEVEN CONSPIRATORS 59
  - DARIUS...62
- **THE PERSIAN EMPIRE**... **64**
  - INDIA...66
  - ARABIA...67
  - EUROPE..68
  - OROETES...69
  - DEMOCEDES 71
  - SYLOSON 73
  - INTAPHERNES 75
  - BABYLONIA REVOLTS 76
- **SCYTHIA** **80**
  - EXPEDITION TO SCYTHIA..85
  - THRACE 86
  - SCYTHIA 87
  - JOURNEY AROUND SCYTHIA 89
  - HISTIAEUS 93
- **EXPEDITION TO ATHENS**... **95**
  - ERETRIA..95
  - BATTLE OF MARATHON 96

- PAROS 99
- LEMNOS 101

XERXES **103**
- THE PERSIAN ARMY MARCHES.............................106
- XERXES WEEPS 108
- COMPOSITION OF THE ARMY 109
- THESSALY 112
- THE GREEKS PREPARE FOR WAR 114
- GELO 116
- FIRST CONTACT 118

THERMOPYLAE **122**
- ARTEMISIUM..128
- THE SACK OF ATHENS...131
- SALAMIS 134
- THE PERSIANS RETREAT 139
- XERXES 141

PLATAEA **143**
- AMOMPHARETUS 152
- DEPARTURE OF THE PERSIAN FLEET....................156
- XERXES IN SARDIS..159

INDEX..**163**

INTRODUCTION

This book is a concise version of the Histories of Herodotus translated from the Ancient Greek by George Rawlinson in 1858. His translation is still in print and published by Everyman, and the full text is also freely available online.

I have seen, at first hand, the education and scholarship required to produce such work and should make it clear that I have no claim to any scholarship myself. I have simply shortened and restyled the text into a more palatable form in the hope of attracting readers who might be daunted by the length of the original. I have maintained the Rawlinson tone and spirit so that the wisdom of Herodotus might shine through and inspire you.

The Histories is an immensely detailed work, which covers geography, myth and folklore, along with what we now call history. Herodotus was the first prose writer of History and he does not follow a linear tale, often taking a detour, as he covers his topic, beginning with the founding of the Lydian empire in 680 BC and ending with the defeat of the Persian expeditionary force in Greece in 479 BC. This concise version follows the sequence of the original, omitting only some large sections of geographical description and much of the detail.

The story opens with King Candaules inviting his lieutenant, Gyges, to marvel at the beauty of his Queen by hiding behind the bedroom door while she undresses. The Queen catches sight of him but keeps quiet and later forces him to kill the King. Together they founded the Lydian empire in what is now Central Turkey. Gyges pacifies the Gods for this murder by making many gifts to the Oracle at Delphi, but his line is cursed and damned to fail after five generations. The Lydians go on to conquer many lands, and their treasury is full, prompting the Lydian King, Croesus, to wonder why the Athenian philosopher Solon does not regard him as the most fortunate of men. Croesus loses his empire to Cyrus the Great after misinterpreting the prophesy that 'a mighty empire will fall' if he attacks the newly established Persian empire. He realises the wisdom of Solon as Cyrus has him placed on a pyre to be burned.

Herodotus treats us to the history of the Medes and to the way in which the Grandson of King Astyages survives exposure on a mountainside as a baby to lead a small army of Persians to take over and then extend the Persian empire, which soon conquers Babylon, and then the Lydians, and becomes the greatest Empire of the day. Cyrus is killed in a war against the Scythian Queen, Tomyris, and we follow the madness of his son, Cambyses, as he conquers Egypt and is replaced by an imposter on the throne after his death. Darius and the seven conspirators manage to wrest back the throne, and we follow a failed campaign into Scythia, seeing the preparations for the invasion of Greece after the loss of the Battle of Marathon against the Athenians in 490 BC.

It is left to Xerxes to march his massive army into Greece, after raising a navy and building a bridge over the Bosphorus to ensure safe passage for his troops into mainland Greece. We see Xerxes weep at the sight of his army when he climbs a mountain to view them more clearly, and we follow the sequence of the invasion as it is halted at Thermopylae by the Spartans and the naval battle is lost to a navy manned predominantly by Athenians. The Persians sack Athens, but the Athenians take refuge in their 'wooden wall' (the navy) and Xerxes returns home without having conquered Greece.

All of this is described for you in detail in the pages that follow. Please enjoy, and I hope that you are encouraged to read the original and other classic texts and encourage you to look at our website for more information and learning materials.

Stamati Crook, Hove, East Sussex. 2012.

LYDIA

I, Herodotus of Halicarnassus, publish these histories as a record of the great and wonderful actions of both the Greeks and Persians in an attempt to document and explain the origins of their conflict.

The Persians claim that the conflict began because of a woman. Phoenician traders, who had been anchored at Argos for a few days, transported Io, the King's daughter, away with them. The Greeks retaliated by abducting Europa, the daughter of the King of Tyre, and, later, Medea, from, Colchis on the River Phasis.

In another generation, Alexander (Paris), the son of Priam, made off with Helen as his prize, citing the Greek abductions as his justification, but the Greeks launched an army and destroyed the kingdom of Priam, which the Persians regarded as an excessive response to a mere abduction.

The Phoenicians themselves are reasonably sure that Io fell in love with the captain of the trading ship and that no abduction took place at all. The Persians now think that the abduction of a woman is a deed carried out by a wicked man, that vengeance for this is pursued by a foolish man, and that to ignore it is the action of a wise man - for surely the women would not have been abducted if they were not willing.

Whatever the cause of the beginnings of the dispute between the Greeks and Asia, I now move away from stories to what I know of the first actual injuries inflicted on the Greeks by the Lydian King Croesus.

GYGES

The lands of Lydia were ruled for more than five hundred years, through twenty-two generations, by an unbroken chain of Heracleids descended from Alcaeus, the child of Hercules and a slave girl owned by Jardanus.

King Candaules loved his wife greatly and delighted in describing her beauty to his loyal bodyguard and lieutenant, Gyges. The King was very eager to prove how beautiful his wife was and persuaded Gyges to stand quietly behind the royal bedroom door so that he could catch sight of the Queen undressing and understand the depth of the King's love. Gyges did so, but the Queen caught sight of him as he was leaving the room and said nothing.

The next day the Queen summoned her faithful guards and asked them to bring Gyges before her. It was considered a sin by the Lydians to be seen naked, and the Queen offered Gyges a choice. He could be killed there and then or he could stand behind the bedroom door that very night and kill the King and become her Lord. Gyges was torn because of his loyalty to the King but stood there that night with the dagger that the Queen herself had placed in his hand and killed the King.

The people of Lydia were distraught at the nature of this regicide, and the Heracleids wanted to take action and restore one of their kindred to the throne. Gyges and the Queen offered to let the Oracle settle the matter and so a procession trooped off to Delphi to see what the Oracle had to say. The Prophetess allowed Gyges to remain King but prophesied that the Heracleids would have their revenge after five generations. So Gyges remained as the new King and reigned for thirty-eight years, and we can see many gold and silver gifts, known as the Gygian Gold, at the Delphic shrine today.

King Gyges attacked Miletus and Smyrna and took the city of Colophon before ending his reign without further warfare. For three generations, the Lydians continued the war with the Milesians and each year took an army and scorched the earth and burnt the crops of the Milesians, leaving only their buildings standing. The Milesians did not have the strength to withstand these attacks, as they had help only from the people of the island of Chios, but in the twelfth year of these attacks a temple of Athena was burned and King Alyattes, the great-grandson of Gyges, fell ill.

Alyattes consulted the Delphic Oracle but was informed that no answer could be given until the temple to Athena had been restored. This came to the attention of Periander of Corinth, who was a good friend of the Milesian King, Thrasybulus, and apprised him of the situation. Thrasybulus knew that Alyattes would come to negotiate and instructed his people to gather together the last of their corn and wine and throw a huge party, which was witnessed by the Lydian messengers who had come to negotiate for permission to rebuild the temple. Alyattes was tricked into thinking that the years of scorching the Milesian crops had been to no avail and agreed a lasting peace with the Milesians. He then built not one, but two, temples to Athena, and promptly recovered from his illness. Alyattes reigned in peace over the land of Lydia for fifty-seven years and, of course, made many more gifts to the Delphic oracle.

ARION

I must tell you a wondrous tale related to Periander, who was a prince of Corinth. A man called Arion was the greatest harpist in the whole of Greece and went to Sicily after many years in Corinth. After a while, having made his fortune, he decided to return and hired a boat manned by Corinthians to bring him home. The crew discovered his riches and offered Arion the choice of being killed or jumping overboard so that they could share his wealth.

Arion begged them, as his last wish, to be allowed to sing a song and, dressed in his musician's robes, sang beautifully to the spellbound crew before jumping overboard. A dolphin saved him and swam with him to dry land, where he was soon welcomed back in Corinth.

Periander could not believe that a Dolphin would save a man and waited for the crew to return and asked them how the famous bard was doing in Sicily. They could not lie when surprised by the living Arion, and today you can find a beautiful statue of a man and a dolphin by the sea near Corinth.

CROESUS

Croesus, the son of Alyattes, came to the Lydian throne at the age of thirty-five and made war on many Greek cities, subjugating first the city of Ephesus and almost all of the Greek cities to the west of the River Halys, including the Lydians, Phrygians, Mysians, Mariandynians, Chalybians, Paphlagonians, Thracians, Carians, Ionians, Dorians, Aeolians and Pamphylians.

Only the strength of the Lycians and Cilicians saved them from having to pay tribute to Croesus, although the Ionians succeeded in signing a treaty with Croesus after he was warned of their plans to attack his navy and avenge transgressions carried out against their Greek brothers on the mainland.

At this time, an Athenian lawmaker called Solon was travelling in the region, having already visited the court of Amasis in Egypt, and came to the court of Croesus, in Sardis. Solon had given the city of Athens a new constitution and had decided to travel for ten years so that the Athenians could not ask him to amend or repeal any of his laws. Croesus received Solon and had his servants show him around his palace and admire his treasuries, which contained vast riches. After a few days, Croesus granted Solon an audience, for Solon was considered one of the wisest men of his age. During their conversation Croesus asked Solon: 'Stranger of Athens, we have heard much of your wisdom and your love of knowledge and your travels through many lands. Tell me, in your great experience, who is the happiest man you have met?' Solon replied: 'Tellus of Athens, Sire'.

Croesus was astonished: 'Pray tell me why you deem Tellus the happiest man who ever lived?' Solon then described how Tellus had lived through flourishing times and had seen his beautiful sons grow up and have children of their own. After a life of comfort, he had a glorious end, dying gallantly in a battle between the Athenians and their neighbours at Eleusis, and receiving a public funeral, with full honours, on the spot where he died.

Croesus, indignant now that Solon had not recognised him as the happiest of all men, asked who he thought was the second happiest of all men. 'Cleobis and Bito', answered Solon: 'They were Argives, brothers who always had enough for their needs and were very strong in body, winning many prizes at the Games. Once there was a great festival in Argos, held to honour the Goddess Hera, but the oxen did not come home in time from the fields to pull their mother's cart for the journey. The two brothers yoked themselves to the cart in which their mother rode and pulled it fully forty-five furlongs to the gates of the temple. Their deed was witnessed by all, and their mother called upon the Goddess to bestow upon them the highest of honours that mortals can attain. That night, after the sacrifice and great banquet, the brothers fell asleep in the temple and never woke again. The Argives built statues to them which they installed in the shrine at Delphi and looked upon them as the best of men'.

Croesus was angry now and demanded of Solon: 'How can it be, Stranger of Athens, that you judge the happiness of private men to be greater than mine?' Solon gave a reply worthy of an Athenian philosopher: 'Sire, you have asked a question regarding the condition of man, and we know that the Gods can become jealous and cause us trouble at any time in our lives. I consider seventy years to be the limit of the life of any man, which I calculate as twenty-six thousand, two hundred and fifty days, any one of which can be full of a variety of events causing happy or unhappy accidents. I see that you are immensely rich and Lord of many nations but I cannot consider you fortunate until you have reached the end of your life happily. Many of the wealthiest men have experienced misfortune, whereas men of moderate means have had excellent luck and happier lives. It is true that a wealthy man is better able to satisfy his desires and is in a stronger position to bear misfortune, but a happy man must be healthy and free from disease and fortunate with his children and be in a position to end his life well. So, we can regard you as fortunate, but not happy, until we see how your life ends, for the Gods often give a man a gleam of happiness before plunging him into ruin'.

ATYS

The King took this answer indifferently, and Solon left without receiving any largesse or honour. Soon afterwards Croesus dreamt that a misfortune would befall one of his sons, who would die by the blow of an iron weapon. Croesus had two sons, one blasted by a natural defect, being deaf and dumb, and the other, Atys, who was above all his friends in every pursuit. Croesus immediately moved all weapons out of the male quarters for fear that one might fall and kill Atys, made arrangements for his marriage and prevented him from accompanying the army into battle or undertaking any activity that might carry any danger for him.

A stranger from Phrygia arrived at this time. This was Adrastus, the grandson of Midas, who had unintentionally slain his brother and was seeking purification. Croesus was a friend to this royal family and gave the Prince hospitality after performing the purification ritual.

Ambassadors soon arrived at court seeking help from Croesus' son to kill a huge monster of a boar that was wasting the cornfields of the Mysians at Mount Olympus. Croesus explained that his son was busy making marriage preparations and offered a select band of Lydians, along with all of his huntsmen and hounds, to help rid the country of this animal.

Atys heard of this quest and persuaded his father to let him go, as the only weapons of the boar were his tusks, whereas the dream had specifically mentioned a blow from an iron weapon. Croesus gave his consent but urged Adrastus to go with the hunting party, watch over his son and make sure that no harm befell him.

The hunting party set out and soon reached Mount Olympus and located the boar. Adrastus hurled his spear at the boar but missed his aim and struck Atys, who was slain by the point of the iron weapon, thus fulfilling the prophecy. The party returned, and Atys was buried, with Adrastus killing himself on the funeral pyre to atone for unwillingly killing both his brother and the son of the man who had given him hospitality and purification.

Croesus was in mourning for his son for two years.

PROPHECY

Toward the end of his mourning, it came to pass that the Persian King Cyrus destroyed the empire of Astyages and was becoming daily more powerful. Croesus decided to consult an Oracle to help him to decide whether it was possible to check this growing power by force before it confronted him. He sent his messengers in different directions to test the Oracles in Greece at Delphi, Dodoma, Abae in Phocis, Amphiaraus, and Trophonius, along with that at Branchidae in Milesia, and the Oracle of Ammon in Libya. The messengers were to count the days since they had left Sardis and consult the Oracles on the hundredth day on what Croesus was doing at that very moment.

The replies came back, but only the Oracle at Delphi has been preserved. This indicated that Croesus was preparing a dish of lamb and tortoise over a fire in a brass pot. Croesus offered a huge sacrifice of three thousand of every kind of sacrificial beast and sent a huge golden statue of a lion to the Oracle, together with two vast bowls, one of gold and one of silver. He also sent his second question: whether he should go to war with the Persians and whether he should strengthen himself with the forces of an ally. The reply came back that, 'if Croesus attacked the Persians, he would, indeed, destroy a mighty empire and he should make an alliance with the most powerful of the Greeks'.

At once he sent his third and final question to the Oracle to discover whether his kingdom would endure. The reply came back that his kingdom would last 'until a mule was crowned monarch of Media'. This pleased Croesus, as it seemed incredible that a mule would become King of the Medes, and he sent his messengers forth to negotiate an alliance with either the Lacedaemonians (Spartans) or the Athenians, whichever were the most powerful of the Greeks.

PISISTRATUS

Croesus soon discovered that the Athenians were in a state of grievous distraction under their tyrant, Pisistratus, the son of Hippocrates. The story is that Hippocrates was once at the Olympic Games, taking part in a sacrificial ritual, when the cauldrons that stood nearby began to boil without the help of any fire, with the water overflowing the pots. Chilon witnessed this omen and advised Hippocrates that he should never take into his house a wife who could bear him a child and, if he already had a wife and child, he should send her back to her father and disown his son. Hippocrates ignored this advice and, sometime afterwards, became the father of Pisistratus.

At a time when Athens was at war, Pisistratus conceived a plan to make himself tyrant of the city by wounding himself and his mule and then driving his chariot into the market place, exclaiming that he had just escaped from his enemies. He persuaded the people to assign him an armed guard of citizens carrying clubs and then broke into the citadel and thus acquired the sovereignty of Athens and became tyrant. Before he could establish himself properly, peace was declared and he was thrown out of Athens.

Megacles, the leader of one of the warring factions, offered Pisistratus his daughter, and together they contrived an extraordinary device to make him tyrant again. They dressed a woman called Phya, who was almost four cubits tall, in armour and drove her, in a chariot, into the city, where heralds proclaimed that the Goddess Athena herself was leading Pisistratus back into the city to reclaim his authority. The people prostrated themselves, and Pisistratus was installed as tyrant for a second time with his new wife.

However, Pisistratus already had a family, and he made sure that there was no possibility of having children with his new wife. Megacles got wind of this, and Pisistratus was forced to flee to Eretria, where the rest of his family lived. They made plans and collected enough money over the next eleven years to return to Marathon, near Athens, with an army of mercenaries. The Athenians mobilised their army and set up camp nearby, upon which Pisistratus, after hearing a prophecy, ordered an immediate attack just after the midday meal, when the

Athenians were relaxing and taking their siesta. The Athenians were routed, and Pisistratus sent his sons ahead toward Athens on horseback to exhort the returning soldiers to be of good cheer and to go back to their homes. Pisistratus thus became tyrant for the third time.

On this occasion, he made sure that he held on to power by keeping enough in the treasury to pay for mercenaries and sending hostages to the island of Naxos, which he had also conquered. This was the state of Athens when the messengers of Croesus investigated the city, with many Athenians fallen in battle and many fled from the city altogether.

LACEDAEMONIANS

The Lacedaemonians (Spartans) were a Doric race who had recently been victorious in a war with the people of Tegea after a period of great tribulation. The Lacedaemonians had been badly governed until their King, Lycurgus, set down a new system of laws, obtained, some said, from the Oracle at Delphi, or, perhaps, from Crete. These Spartans built a temple to Lycurgus. They prospered and regarded all others as their inferiors. After consulting the Oracle, which recommended that they avoid conflict with the Arcadians, they set about a war designed to enslave the Tegeans. After many defeats and lost battles, the Kings Anaxandrides and Aristo began to make changes in a manner which I shall relate to you.

After losing every engagement with the Tegeans, they sent to the Oracle at Delphi, and the Pythoness told them that they must obtain the bones of Orestes, the son of Agamemnon, before they might find fortune in war. The bones could not be found despite years of searching until, during a fragile peace, a Spartan called Lichas, who was travelling in Tegea, heard a blacksmith mention that he had come across a huge coffin seven cubits long when he had been digging for a well in his workshop.

The Spartan returned to his homeland, where a plan was conceived and a fraudulent prosecution instigated, after which he was banished. Lichas pretended to flee Sparta for Tegea and, having related his misfortune to the blacksmith, rented a room in the workshop. Soon afterwards, Lichas dug down and retrieved the bones, bringing them to Sparta, and, in the wake of this, the Spartans had nothing but victories. By the time the messengers of Croesus came to investigate, they were masters of most of the Peloponnese.

Croesus was now in a position to make his decision and sent messengers to Sparta with gifts in their hands to request an alliance. The Spartans were already aware of the messages that the Oracle had given Croesus and were well disposed toward the Lydians, and particularly pleased to have been chosen in preference to all other Greeks. As a consequence, they formed the alliance, waited in readiness for a summons and sent a great vase made of bronze by ship to Sardis. This, however, never arrived because, according to the Spartans, the people of Samos stole it *en route*.

LYDIANS AND MEDES

Meanwhile, Croesus had already led his forces into Cappadocia, fully expecting to defeat Cyrus and destroy the Persians despite the warnings of a wise Lydian, called Sandanis, who wondered what Croesus might gain from attacking the Persians. For the Persians had nothing and, once they understood the riches of Croesus, they would always be of a mind to conquer the Lydians, whereas they had not, so far, thought of this. Croesus coveted the land of Cappadocia and wanted revenge against the conqueror of Astyages, who was his brother by marriage, the circumstances of which I must relate to you now.

Cyaxares, the King of the Medes and father of Astyages, had come across a band of Scythian nomads and had allowed them to settle. He had entrusted a number of boys into their care to whom they were to teach their language and the use of the bow. The Scythians were accustomed to hunting but one day returned with nothing, receiving the fury of Cyaxares, who was hot-tempered and presumably very hungry. The Scythians were greatly offended and resolved to cut one of the boys up into pieces and dress the flesh up as game and serve it to the King, which they promptly did before fleeing to Sardis, and the Lydians.

Alyattes, King of the Lydians, refused to give up the Scythians to the Medes, and a war broke out, with many victories on each side. In the sixth year of the war, the day turned, all of a sudden, to night during the course of a battle. This event had been predicted to the Ionians by Thales, a Milesian, but the Lydians and the Medes stopped fighting and agreed a peace sealed by the marriage of the daughter of Alyattes to Astyages, the son of Cyaxares.

CAPPADOCIA

Croesus crossed the river Halys with help, some say, from Thales the Milesian, who succeeded in diverting the river on either side of the army to allow them to construct a ford across each half. Once in Cappadocia, he took the main city, Pteria, reducing the inhabitants to slavery, and made himself master of the region.

Cyrus already held Astyages prisoner and marched his army toward Croesus, picking up more troops with each nation through which he passed. Croesus had asked the Ionians for aid but had been refused and met with Cyrus in the region of Pteria. Both sides fought valiantly, and many were slain. The next day Croesus realised that he was short of troops and returned to Sardis, invoking his alliances with the Egyptians, and the Babylonians, and urging the Lacedaemonians to help to supply him with more troops. He arranged go assemble this army in five months and, in the meantime, he disbanded his existing militia, never imagining that Cyrus would dare march on Sardis.

Cyrus, however, marched his army right up to the walls of Sardis, and Croesus had no choice but to lead his army out to meet him on the plain. As Cyrus beheld the Lydian army assembling and preparing for battle there, he grew fearful of the Lydian cavalry and adopted a strategy suggested to him by Harpargus, one of the Medes. He gathered together all of the camels which had been serving as pack animals, mounted riders upon them and ordered them to advance in front of his troops against the Lydian cavalry. The Lydian horses were scared by the scent of the camels, upon which the cavalry were forced to leap off their horses and fight on foot. A great slaughter ensued, after which the Persians surrounded the city and began the siege of Sardis. Croesus now sent messengers to his allies, including the Spartans, asking that they come at once, as he was already besieged.

THYREA

At this time, the Spartans were in a dispute with the Argives, after the former had seized a place called Thyrea, and came to terms before any battle was fought, by agreeing that a force of three hundred Spartans would face three hundred Argives and fight to settle the dispute.

The armies departed, leaving the six hundred men to fight the battle.

At the end of the day, just three men were left standing: two Argives, called Alcanor and Chromius, and a single Spartan called Othryadas. The Argives departed to declare themselves victorious, whereas the Spartans stayed behind, stripping the fallen of their armour before returning to their camp. In the morning, the sides met but were unable to agree which had won, upon which they fell to arms and many were slain, although the Lacedaemonians prevailed in this battle.

In the wake of their defeat, the Argives cut their hair short, and vowed to keep it short, and forbid their womenfolk from wearing gold, until Thyrea had been recaptured. Conversely, the Lacedaemonians swore to wear their hair long, despite the fact that they had, in the past, always cut it close. Othryadas, as the sole survivor of the three hundred, became ashamed and killed himself. Despite this preoccupation, the Spartans prepared to depart and honour their allegiance to the Lydians. However, they received news that Sardis had been taken and Croesus captured by the Persians.

SIEGE OF SARDIS

On the fourteenth day of the siege, Cyrus issued a proclamation that a great reward would be offered to the first man who could scale the walls of Sardis. One side of the citadel had a sheer precipice which looked absolutely secure, but a Mardian called Hyroeades had seen a Lydian soldier descend the rock while chasing after a helmet that had rolled down from the top. The next day he climbed the rock himself with a number of other Persians until a large number had gathered and the Persians thus took the city.

Remember the son of Croesus who was a worthy youth but who had an affliction and was deaf and dumb? Croesus had sent to the Oracle at Delphi some time past and had been told that it might be wise to listen to the boy's unintelligible sounds and woe betide the day when his ear should first hear his son's words. During the pillage of Sardis, a Persian soldier was about to kill Croesus, not knowing who he was, and Croesus' son, in the agony of his fear and grief, burst forth into speech and said: 'Do not kill Croesus'. Thus, Croesus was taken prisoner and his son retained the power of speech for the rest of his life.

So, in the fourteenth year of his reign and after fourteen days of the siege, Croesus fulfilled the prophecy of the Oracle, which said that he would destroy a mighty empire - by destroying his own!

Cyrus built a great pyre and placed Croesus upon it and set it alight. As the flames took hold, Croesus remembered the words of Solon and cried out his name three times. Cyrus heard the sounds and bade his interpreters discover his meaning and was told how Solon had seen the treasures of Croesus and made light of his splendours and that everything he had said regarding the happiness of man had come to be. Cyrus was moved and realised that Croesus had once been a man of great fortune like himself and gave orders to cut him down. His men, however, could not quench the blaze, and, as he began to burn, Croesus called out to Apollo and the sky immediately darkened and a storm burst out and put out the flames. Cyrus was now convinced that Croesus was blessed and asked who had persuaded him to attack and become his enemy. Croesus replied: 'The God of the Greeks persuaded me, as no one should be foolish enough to prefer war to peace, where fathers bury their sons instead of sons burying their fathers'.

After a moment, Croesus indicated that he would like to address Cyrus: 'What is it that your men are doing so busily?' 'Plundering your city', replied Cyrus with satisfaction. 'But it is not my city', rejoined Croesus 'It is now your city they are plundering'. Croesus advised Cyrus that his people had once enjoyed great wealth, and that Cyrus could expect the most powerful of them to attempt to depose him, and so they hatched plans to have the bodyguard search the Persian soldiers as they left the city and limit their riches by persuading them to make offerings to Zeus with a portion of their booty.

Cyrus was pleased and asked Croesus what reward he desired, whereupon messengers were sent to the Oracle at Delphi to enquire why he had been encouraged to begin a war with Persia and destroy his own empire despite being faithful to the gods. The Oracle informed Croesus that Apollo was, indeed, on his side and had delayed his defeat by a full three years and had, furthermore, saved him from the burning pyre. However, the God was unable to persuade the Fates not to destroy him, as he was the fifth ancestor of a bodyguard of the Heracleids who had joined in a woman's fraud and wrongfully seized the throne from his master. Furthermore, Croesus should have enquired further after receiving the message that he was to destroy an empire, to discover which empire would be destroyed and finally, it was said that Cyrus was the mule, as his mother was a Median princess, daughter of King Astyages, and his father a Persian, and thus correctly prophesied to become King.

So it was that Ionia was first conquered by the Persians and the empire of Croesus came to an end.

LYDIA

Lydia does not have very many attributes for a historian to describe. There is, however, the great tomb of Alyattes, adjacent to Lake Gygaea, built by all of the handymen and tradesmen of Sardis, and paid for by the courtesans. The Lydians have many customs similar to those of the Greeks and were the first to strike coins and have shops at which goods were exchanged for money. They are said to have invented games such as dice and ball as a means of forgetting the hunger brought on by a long famine. This lasted eighteen years, and half the population had to leave Smyrna to found a new people called the Tyrrhenians.

CYRUS THE GREAT

The Assyrians of Upper Asia had held power for five hundred and twenty years when a revolt, begun by the Medes, resulted in all of their subject nations gaining self-government.

One of the Medes, called Deioces, set himself the task of becoming King, as the Medes had no central authority and lawlessness prevailed. He was already a respected and powerful man and devoted himself to resolving disputes and becoming an upright and honest judge and was consulted on all of the quarrels and disputes which arose until, at last, the people had confidence in no one but him.

At this point, Deioces decided to devote himself to his own interests and no longer sat and administered justice, until the people, many of them his friends, beseeched him to prevent the lawlessness that had broken out again. The people decided to choose a King and named Deioces, who demanded a palace and a bodyguard, commanding that the city of Agbatana be built and that the Medes abandon their villages to live in the great city.

Once the city had been completed and great protective walls built, he allowed no one direct access to the King and forbade his subjects to look upon him or to laugh or spit in the royal presence. Deioces thought that, if his friends could gaze upon him they might realise that he was like them and might be pained because of his glory and would conspire against him, whereas if they did not see him they might think him a different sort of being from themselves. So Deioces became King of the Medes and continued to administer justice, and he set up spies and messengers so that he could punish anyone guilty of conspiring against him.

Deioces reigned for fifty-three years and was succeeded by his son Phraortes, who reigned for twenty-two years and attacked the Persians, bringing them under the Medean yoke. He also attacked the Assyrians, the former lords of Asia, but was defeated and killed, with the greater part of his army, and succeeded by his son, Cyaxares.

CYAXARES

Cyaxares was even more warlike and organised his army into companies, with distinct bodies of spearmen, archers and cavalry, and brought under his dominion the whole of Asia beyond the River Halys. It was Cyaxares who had fought the Lydians when the day had changed into night.

Cyaxares gathered the troops of the many nations he had conquered and waged war on the Assyrians at Nineveh, hoping to avenge his father, but a horde of Scythians, under their King Madyes, invaded Medea and engaged in battle. They defeated the Medes and become the masters of Asia. The Scythians continued through Syria on to Egypt, where they were persuaded by the Egyptian King, Psammetichus, to advance no further and contented themselves with an insolent and oppressive rule over Asia for twenty-eight years.

Cyaxares and the Medes paid tribute to the Scythians but finally decided to revolt and invited the greater part of the Scythians to a banquet, massacred them, regained their empire and took Nineveh and conquered all of Assyria apart from the region of Babylonia.

ASTYAGES

Cyaxares reigned for forty years, if we include the time of the Scythians, and his son Astyages succeeded to the throne. Astyages had a dream in which his daughter, Mandane, urinated in such quantity that the whole of Asia was flooded, and, consequently, after taking advice from the oracles, he decided that he could not marry her to a Mede and married her to a Persian of good family called Cambyses. Astyages then had another dream, in which a vine grew out of his daughter and cast the whole of Asia into shadow, which, according to the Oracle, indicated that the offspring of his daughter would reign over Asia in his stead.

In due course, his daughter became pregnant and Astyages ordered his loyal relative Harpargus to kill the child as soon as he was born. Harpargus visited the house and saw the newborn child, called Cyrus, but as soon as the baby was delivered into his hands, dressed in funeral clothes, he wept as he could not in conscience kill his own kin. So he sent for the herdsman Mitradates and ordered him, under pain of death, to take the child into the mountains and expose him to the elements. Now it happened that the wife of Mitradates was expecting a baby, and he discovered on his return home that his infant had been stillborn, and so the couple decided to switch babies so their dead child would have a royal funeral and that Cyrus might live.

I shall now relate the story of how the identity of Cyrus was discovered by accident when he was ten years old.

He was playing a game with other boys one day: they had elected him King in their game, and he had set some boys to build him houses, others as guards, others as messengers, and so on. Among the boys was the son of a noble who refused to carry out the tasks that Cyrus had set him. Cyrus ordered the other boys to arrest him and submit him to a whipping. The boy complained to his father, a noble called Artembares, that the son of a cowherd had mistreated him. Artembares complained to Astyages and so, Cyrus was called into the presence of the King.

Astyages admonished the young Cyrus for behaving so rudely to the son of a noble, but Cyrus replied that the other boys had chosen him to be the King and that all these boys had done as ordered, with only the son of Artembares refusing to submit to his authority. Astyages was impressed by the manner of this reply and, sensing some physical likenesses to himself, began to question the cowherd. The cowherd at first claimed that Cyrus was his own son but soon told the truth as the guards grabbed him and dragged him toward the rack. Although Astyages was very angry once he had discovered the truth, he remained calm and called for Harpargus, who, once he saw Cyrus and recognised the cowherd standing there, admitted that he had ordered the cowherd to kill the baby. He asserted that he had not told a lie, as his guards had seen that the baby had been exposed and had died after a few days. Astyages was still angry but kept calm and indicated to Harpargus that he was happy that his grandson had survived and bid Harpargus send over his son to play with Cyrus and that he attend dinner that evening.

As soon as the son of Harpargus arrived, Astyages had him seized and chopped into pieces and a meal prepared from the flesh with the head and hands covered up and placed in a basket. The King served the flesh to Harpargus during the meal that evening, whereas the rest of the dinner party fed on the usual fare. Astyages asked Harpargus how he had enjoyed the meal, and the latter replied that he had enjoyed the meal excessively, upon which the basket was brought forth and the remains of his son revealed to him. Harpargus kept his composure and indicated that whatever the King did was agreeable to him before collecting all the remaining flesh together to leave and, I suppose, go and bury his son.

Astyages then consulted the Magi for guidance on what to do with Cyrus. They all countenanced that the young Cyrus had already been made King by the boys in the village, and the prophecy had, therefore, been fulfilled. Astyages had little to fear from the young Cyrus but better to exile him than allow for the possibility of a half-Persian becoming King of the Medes. Astyages therefore sent his grandson off to Persia to live with his real mother, who was overjoyed and very surprised to see him again, and Cyrus grew to be one of the bravest and most popular of his peers.

PERSIA REVOLTS

Meanwhile, Harpargus had been plotting revenge on Astyages for the murder of his son and had already persuaded several of the Medean nobles who had their own quarrels with the King to join his cause. He saw that the best plan would be for an open revolt, with the aim of making Cyrus the new King and contrived to get a message to the young Cyrus by placing a letter inside a hare. He disguised his most loyal servant as a hunter and sent him to Persia with the game as a present to Cyrus, bidding him to prepare the animal himself for the table. So, Cyrus received the letter which read as follows: 'Son of Cambyses. Surely the Gods watch over thee, for you have passed through many adventures and yet remain fortunate. You know what I have suffered because I put you into the hands of a cowherd instead of killing you as a baby. Please listen now and all the empire of Astyages will be yours. You must raise a revolt in Persia and march straight on the land of the Medes and worry not. Whether Astyages appoints me or one of the other nobles in command of the forces drawn up against you, expect them to melt away and change sides and join you at the first opportunity. So do your part speedily'.

Cyrus quickly contrived a plan and called forth all of the Persians of the leading tribes and pretended to read from a scroll that Astyages had appointed him General of the Persians and that they should all gather the next day and each man bring his reaping hook. The menfolk assembled on the next day, and their new General pointed to a large tract of land, covered in great thorny bushes, and ordered them to clear this. They toiled hard all day and finished the task just before nightfall, whereupon they were ordered home to bathe and instructed to return on the following day. Meanwhile, Cyrus ordered all of his father's goats and sheep slaughtered and prepared a great feast, along with wine and bread of the choicest kind. The next day Cyrus hosted a great feast for the whole army and then questioned the men after the feast was over as to which day's work they had preferred. All of them answered that the days were of extreme contrast and that 'yesterday brought them everything that was bad and today everything that was good'. Cyrus seized on these words and urged them to revolt. 'If you listen to my words you can enjoy ten thousand such delights and never have to slave again, so follow me and be free for I am destined to undertake your liberation. Revolt against the Medes without delay and follow me'.

Astyages discovered the imminent revolt and ordered Cyrus into his presence, but Cyrus sent messengers to him, saying that he would see him sooner than he would like, and so the Persians marched against the Medes. As if deprived of his senses, Astyages made

Harpargus his general and, as a result, his forces abandoned him when drawn up against the Persians. Astyages called out the townsfolk and fought a battle during which he was utterly defeated and taken prisoner. Harpargus found Astyages captive and gloated that he had arranged his downfall and could take the credit for the successful revolt. 'More fool you', replied Astyages, 'for why did you not put yourself on the throne if you had this power, instead of a Persian who will make slaves of the Medes and Lords of the Persians'.

Thus did Astyages lose his throne after thirty-five years and the Persians gain dominion of the parts of Asia beyond the Halys. Cyrus kept Astyages by his side and went on to conquer Lydia, as we have already heard, becoming master of all Asia and creating an empire that lasted one hundred and twenty-eight years (apart from the time of the Scythians).

PERSIANS

The Persians do not think of the Gods in their own image and offer sacrifice to one God, and also to the sun, moon, earth, fire, water and the winds. They have no images of the gods and no temples or altars and consider their use a folly. They do not raise a fire or pour libations or play music during a sacrifice but find a clean spot of ground, and the priest, wearing a wreath of myrtle around his head, calls upon God on behalf of the King and the whole Persian people. The animal is slaughtered and boiled and a Magus called upon to chant a hymn after which they can make use of the flesh in any way they please.

Persians love to celebrate their birthday, and the richer classes will bake a whole camel, ox, horse or ass, while the poorer classes use a cow. They eat only a little solid food and a large number of desserts and it is not their custom to vomit or go to the toilet in the presence of another. They usually make decisions on important matters when they are drunk and then reconsider the decision when they are sober. Sometimes they are sober when they make decisions but they always make sure to reconsider the matter when drunk to see if they come to the same conclusion.

People of equal rank greet each other with a kiss on the lips but those of different rank with a kiss given on the cheek. If there is a great difference in rank then the inferior will prostrate himself on the ground. They honour most their neighbouring nations and those furthest from their borders least, probably because they think themselves so much better than all of mankind, and thus believe that those who live the furthest away from them must be the most degraded.

Persians are quick to adopt the habits of foreign peoples and they dress in the manner of the Medes and wear Egyptian breastplates as armour in war. They adopt any luxury as they come across it and have learnt their love of boys from the Greeks and have several wives and even more concubines. After fighting, the greatest merit is given to the fathers of many sons, and each year the King sends gifts accordingly. Their sons are carefully instructed from the age of five in just three things: to ride, draw a bow, and to speak the truth. They spend their first five years without seeing their fathers so that the father is not distressed if the child dies young.

No Persian can be put to death for a single fault and in the case of a slave being considered for the extreme penalty, all of their good services are taken into account and they are pardoned if their good deeds outweigh the bad. A Persian has never killed his father or mother, and they consider it unlawful even to talk about unlawful things. After telling a lie, the next worst thing is to owe a debt in business, and if a Persian develops leprosy, he is seen to have sinned against the sun and exiled.

All of this I can tell you from my own knowledge, but I have also heard that no male Persian is buried until his corpse has been torn by either a dog or a bird of prey. The dead bodies are then covered in wax and buried in the ground. Their priests or Magi kill all sorts of animals with their own hands, excepting dogs and men, in contrast to the Egyptian priests, who never kill any live animals apart from those offered in sacrifice.

Now, however, I must return to my story.

IONIANS

Of the many Ionian city states, only the Milesians were in an alliance with Persia. Immediately after the conquest of Lydia, Cyrus received deputations from many Ionian and Aeolian Greeks who wanted to be his lieges as they had been under Croesus. Cyrus listened attentively but then refused their request, citing a parable: 'There was a piper who played his pipes by the sea expecting the fish to jump out of the water and come to him on the land. He tried in vain and then took a net and drew a great number of fish ashore. The fish began to leap and dance but the piper asked them to cease their dancing as they had chosen not to dance when he piped to them before'.

The Spartans also sent a deputation to Cyrus, warning him not to molest any of the cities of Greece, but Cyrus replied that 'The Spartans will have enough troubles of their own if I live and should not concern themselves over the troubles of the Ionians'. So Cyrus left Sardis under the charge of a Persian called Tabalus and proceeded to the city of Agbatana to make war on the Babylonians, the Bactrians, the Scythians and the

Egyptians, leaving to one of his generals the task of conquering the Ionians.

As soon as he had left Sardis, a Mede called Pactyas, who had been entrusted with gathering together the treasures of Croesus, rebelled and used the vast treasures at his disposal to raise an army of mercenaries. Cyrus consulted Croesus, who was travelling with him, and was of a mind to slaughter and enslave the Lydians. Croesus suggested that he deal with those Lydians who had risen in revolt and forbid the remainder from carrying arms and bade them bring up their sons to play the harp and to be shopkeepers, so that there would be no fear of a revolt in the future. Cyrus liked what he heard and gave orders to a Mede called Mazares, who returned to Sardis and implemented the policies, after Pactyas had fled with his army. Mazares eventually took custody of Pactyas from the people of the island of Chios and enslaved one of the Medean cities which had risen in revolt, whereupon Mazares suddenly sickened and died.

Harpargus, the man to whom Astyages had fed the unholy banquet, succeeded to his command and took many cities of Ionia by means of piling mounds of earth against the city walls. The first city to be besieged was Phocaea, which had a great wall surrounding it. Harpargus offered them terms, and they asked for a day to reply and took their wives and children and wealth, and even their images of their gods, and set sail for Chios, where they attempted to negotiate the purchase of some islands to make their city anew. The Chians refused, and the Phocaeans set sail for Corsica but first revisited their city and put the Persian garrison to the sword. Half their number decided to stay in their city, and the other half settled in Corsica, but, after five years, lost most of their ships in a great sea battle with their neighbours and had to move on and settle in Rhegium, where they founded the city of Velia.

A similar fate befell the townspeople of Teos, who set sail across the sea to Thrace and founded the city of Abdera, after Harpargus had raised his mound to the height of their defences. The remaining city states fought valiantly to defend their cities but were defeated one by one by the forces of Harpargus. Thus were the continental Ionians reduced to servitude, and many of the Ionians of the islands also gave themselves up to Cyrus. Harpargus forced the Ionians and Aeolians to serve in his army and went on to attack and conquer the Carians, the Caunians and the Lycians.

BABYLON

Meanwhile, Cyrus had secured many victories and was conquering most of upper Asia. I will not go into the detail of his successful conquests, except to tell you how Cyrus made war on the Assyrians, who possessed a vast number of cities, including the city of Babylon, which was the most renowned and the strongest.

The city stands on a plain and stretches for one hundred and twenty furlongs on each side, with its walls forming a perfect square surrounded by a deep moat. When the Assyrians were digging the moat, they baked the earth they dug out into bricks and used them to line the moat and build a wall two hundred royal cubits high and fifty royal cubits wide (a royal cubit is three fingers' width longer than a standard cubit). Along the top of the wall they built single chambers facing each other with room for a four-horsed chariot to turn. A river divides the city into two, and its banks are lined with brick and one hundred brass gates with brass lintels and gateposts lining the walls. Most of the houses are three or four storeys high, with the streets running in straight lines and a brass gate at the end of each street, where it meets the water.

There is a second defensive wall, and a sacred temple is to be found in the middle of the city, a solid mass of masonry one furlong on each side, raised up into a tower, upon which is set a second tower, and so on, up to the eighth tower, and this structure was still standing in my time. A path around the outside of the tower leads up to a spacious temple in the topmost tower which has no statues of any kind and an unusually large couch, richly adorned, with a golden table by its side. A solitary woman occupies the chamber, and it is said that the god comes down in person each night and sleeps there. There was a second temple in the time of Cyrus, which I have not seen, with a single golden figure of Zeus sitting down at a golden table and, outside, two altars, one of solid gold, upon which animals are sacrificed.

One of the Queens of the Assyrians, named Nitocris, had seen the tremendous power and restless enterprise of the Medes and taken great steps to fortify the city, as I shall now describe. She excavated the River Euphrates upstream of the city and caused it to deviate, such that it flowed within sight of a village called Ardericea at three separate places. She had a huge lake dug out and built embankments along the river to render navigation difficult and discourage intercourse between the Medes and the Babylonians and thus keep them in ignorance of her affairs. She also diverted the river for a time and built a series of pontoons and gates along the banks within the city to allow wooden platforms to be laid across for the townspeople to cross during the day. These would be removed at night to stop people passing from side to side in the dark to commit robberies. She also built her tomb high above the heads of the passersby in one of these gates with the inscription: 'If one of my successors on the throne of Babylon finds themselves truly in need, let them open my tomb and take as much as they choose'. The tomb remained untouched until the time of Darius, and he found just the dead body without any treasure, and a second inscription: 'If thou were not insatiate of self, thou would not have broken open the sepulchres of the dead'.

Cyrus was at war with Labynetus, the son of Nitocris, who was King of the Assyrians. The Great King Cyrus always travelled with his own cattle, and his food ready prepared from home and water taken with him from the river Choaspes, which is the only water fit for the Kings of Persia to taste. As the Persians were crossing the River Tigris, one of the sacred white horses that accompanied the army tried to swim across the river and drowned. Cyrus was so enraged with the insolence of the river that he caused his army to delay for most of the summer, building one hundred and eighty trenches on each side of the river to break its strength, so that even women could cross it easily without wetting their knees. He approached Babylon in the spring and fought and defeated the Babylonian army, which was waiting for him outside the gates a short distance from the city. The Babylonians then locked themselves in the city and made light of the siege, as they had stored enough food to survive for many years.

Cyrus made no progress but, after a certain amount of time, he conceived a plan and divided his army into two, leaving one half at the point at which the river entered the city and the other half at the point where it issued forth. He then took the non-combatant part of his army and used the basin already dug by Nitocris to divert the river once more. The Babylonians could have defeated the Persians had they guarded all the gates lining the river in the city, but they were caught by surprise, as the Persians breached the city once the level of the waters had fallen. Such was the size of the city that the people in the middle of the town knew nothing until it had been captured.

BABYLONIANS

The Persians call their provinces a satrapy, and the satrapy of the Babylonians is the largest and most powerful of all the satrapies, yielding a third of all of the tribute of the empire.

Only a little rain falls in Assyria, but enough to make the corn sprout, and irrigation is used to help the corn to grow. The whole of Babylonia is crisscrossed with irrigation canals, and we know of no country which is more fruitful in yielding grain, commonly two-hundredfold and sometimes three-hundredfold. The blade of the wheat and barley plant is often four fingers in breadth, and the millet and sesame grow to a great height which must seem incredible if you have never visited the area. The only oil they use is from the sesame plant, and they do not grow figs, olives, vines or any other kind of tree. They do grow palm trees which bear fruit, and this fruit supplies them with bread, wine and honey.

One thing that surprises me most about Babylonia are the boats which come down the river to Babylon. These are round and made of skin. Each carries two men and a cargo, usually of wine, along with an ass. Once the cargo has been landed and sold, the men dismantle and pack up the boat, load the ass and return on foot, as the current is too strong for the boat to return upstream.

Babylonians have long hair and wear turbans on their heads, anointing their entire body with perfume. They wear a long linen tunic reaching down to their feet, with a woollen fabric over this. They sport a short white cloak and carry a seal and a walking stick, usually with a decoration such as a flower or eagle carved upon it. Each year they garner in all the maidens who are to be married, and these are offered for sale with the most beautiful going to the highest bidder. The money raised is used to create a dowry for the uglier or crippled women who, thus subsidised, might find a man to marry. The Babylonians have no doctors but bring out the sick into a public square and passers-by come up and give advice if any of them have previously suffered the same ailment. The dead are buried in honey with funeral lamentations, like the Egyptians, and when a Babylonian has consorted with his wife, they clean themselves with incense and will not touch any utensils until they have washed, a practice also observed by the Arabians.

The Babylonians have a shameful custom by which every woman must, once in her lifetime, go and sit in the precinct of Aphrodite and wait for a man to throw a silver coin into her lap and she cannot refuse to go with him, for once he has thrown the coin it becomes sacred. Once she has gone with the man, she has satisfied the goddess and can return home, and from then onwards, no amount of money can prevail upon her. Some of the less beautiful women might wait three or four years in the precinct. A similar practice is found in certain parts of the island of Cyprus.

QUEEN TOMYRIS

Once Cyrus had conquered Babylon, he desired to bring the Massagetae, a Scythian people, to the east beyond the river Araxes, under his dominion. This river flows into the Caspian Sea, which is frequented by the Greeks and is fifteen days' voyage in a row-boat and eight days in width at its broadest part. The Caspian Sea is bordered by the Caucasus mountains in the west and a vast plain in the east which is inhabited by the Massagetae, against whom Cyrus was so anxious to make an expedition. His motivation seems to have been driven by the circumstances of his birth and his good fortune in all of his previous wars, as it seemed that it was impossible for any country to escape defeat.

The Massagetae fight both on horseback and on foot with bows and lances, but their favourite weapon is the battle axe. They make their arrow points and spear points out of brass but use gold for their headgear and girdles. Each man has one wife, but these are held in common, in such a way that, when a man wants a woman, he hangs a quiver in front of her wagon and lives with her without fear. Human life does not come to a natural close, and when a man grows old, his kinsfolk offer him up in sacrifice together with some cattle and then boil the flesh and feast upon it, and those who end their lives like this are reckoned the happiest. A man who dies of disease is not eaten but is buried in the ground. They sow no grain but live off their herds and fish, which are plentiful in the river Araxes, and they chiefly drink milk. Their only god is the sun, and, to him, they offer the swiftest of animals, the horse, as a sacrifice.

Cyrus sent ambassadors to Tomyris, the Queen of the Massagetae, asking for her hand in marriage. She refused to see his ambassadors and, because of this, Cyrus began to build towers and a bridge to allow his army across the river to give battle. Tomyris, then sent word that it was pointless to spend time bridge building and that she was happy to retire three days' distance and let him cross the river, or for his army to retire three days' distance for her army to cross and engage in battle. Cyrus was advised to let her cross, but Croesus suggested that he choose to cross instead, for, if he lost the battle, the Massagetae would surely follow up their victory and attack his empire, whereas, if he won, he could quickly push on into the heart of their country. Cyrus took this advice and sent his son, Cambyses, back into Persia with Croesus, having advised him to treat Croesus with respect should the expedition fail, and Cyrus took his army across the river.

That night Cyrus had a dream that Darius, the eldest son of Hystaspes, who was just twenty years old and not old enough to come to war, had grown wings, one of which covered Europe and the other Asia. Cyrus was accustomed to warnings from the gods of danger and sent Hystaspes back to Persia to have his son ready to be examined on his return. Cyrus had misread the true nature of the dream, for he was to die then and there, with his kingdom falling at last to Darius.

Cyrus advanced a day's march, leaving the non-combatant troops behind at camp, where they were discovered by a one-third part of the army of the Massagetae led by Spargapises, the son of the Queen, who put them to the sword. They then, seeing a banquet prepared, as suggested by Croesus, indulged themselves in feasting. Cyrus arrived once they had eaten and drunk their full and slaughtered a great number, and took many prisoners, including Spargapises. Now Queen Tomyris sent a message: 'Do not take pride, bloodthirsty Cyrus, in this victory, for it was the grape juice which makes you go mad when you drink it, and it was that poison which let you ensnare my child and it was not a fair fight. Now release him to me and depart, satisfied that you have beaten one-third of my army. Refuse and I swear that I will give you your fill of blood'. Cyrus paid no attention to these words and when Spargapises sobered up and saw the extent of his calamity, he asked for his bonds to be released and destroyed himself.

The Queen then took her forces and engaged the enemy. The two armies shot their arrows for some time, and then closed and fought hand-to-hand with lances and daggers, and continued to fight until, at last, the Massagetae prevailed and the greater part of the Persian army was destroyed, and Cyrus himself fell. A search was made for the body and, when it was found, the Queen took a wineskin and filled it with human blood and dipped the head of the Great King into the gore, saying: 'I have lived and conquered you and make good my threat and give you your fill of blood'. Of the many different accounts I have heard of the death of Cyrus, this is the one to which I give the most credit.

EGYPT

The Egyptians believe themselves to be the most ancient of the races of mankind, and King Psammetichus set out to discover if this were true by raising two newborn children away from the company of man to see what words they might speak when they grew out of infancy.

The children were raised by a goatherd and brought up with goats to provide them with milk, and no one was to utter a word in their presence. After two years, the goatherd noticed that both children uttered the word 'becos' whenever he visited them and that the word was constantly in their mouths. They were brought into the presence of King Psammetichus, whereupon it was discovered that 'becos' was the Phrygian name for bread. Thus it was discovered that, although the Egyptians surpassed all nations, the Phrygians surpass them in antiquity.

I myself went to Heliopolis and to Thebes and spoke with the priests there about many things, including many secrets of their religion which I am not able to divulge here. They told me that the Egyptians were the first to discover the solar year and that they divide the year into twelve months, each of thirty days, and add five days so that the seasons can return at the same time each year. They also brought into use the names of the twelve gods which were later adopted by the Greeks and were the first to erect altars, images, and temples to the gods, and to engrave upon stone the figures of animals.

They told me that the first man to rule Egypt was called Men, and that, in his time, the whole of Egypt was a marsh, with none of the land below Lake Moeris showing itself above water. You can see, as you travel through it, that Egypt is an acquired country, the gift of the river, and you can let down a sounding line even a day's sailing time from the land and find soil washed down from the river there. The coastline of Egypt extends three thousand six hundred furlongs and inland to Heliopolis, which is a distance of fifteen hundred furlongs. The land is flat, without springs, and full of swamps.

It is fifteen hundred furlongs from the sea to Heliopolis and four days travel up country from there where Egypt becomes narrow, shut in by the Arabian hills on one side and the Libyan range on the other. The Arabian range is two months' journey from east to west and stretches away to the Erythraean sea where the quarries that produced stone for the pyramids of Memphis are located, with areas that produce Frankincense at the extreme eastern end. The other ridge is the Libyan range, where the pyramids stand, and this is rocky and covered with sand. At the narrowest point, no more than two hundred furlongs separate the two ranges. It is nine days' travel from Heliopolis to Thebes, a distance of almost five thousand furlongs, and a further eighteen hundred furlongs to Elephantine.

NILE

The Egyptians obtain the fruits of the land with less difficulty than any other people in the world, for they have no need to break up the ground with a plough, or use the hoe, nor do any of the other work which the rest of mankind find necessary if they are to obtain a crop. The farmer waits until the river has spread itself over the fields and withdrawn again before sowing, after which swine are released onto the fields to tread in the corn. On hearing that the land in Greece is watered from the heavens and not by the river, the Egyptians observed that 'the Greeks have nothing to rely on but rain from Zeus and one day may be swept away by famine as they have no other source of water'.

The Nile begins to rise at the summer solstice, and this continues for a hundred days, from which point it recedes and remains low all winter. The Greeks have several explanations for this phenomenon, including theories that the Etesian winds prevent the water from running off into the sea or that the Nile flows from an Ocean that itself flows around the earth. However, both of these views are unscientific, as the river still swells in years in which there are no winds, and there is no river called an ocean. Another idea is that the river is swollen from melted snow, but the water in question comes from some of the hottest parts of the earth and this theory is, therefore, unfeasible. My view is that the path of the sun is diverted during the winter months over the upper parts of Libya and that it draws out water from the river during the winter which it replenishes in the summer.

A scribe I have met describes one of the sources of the Nile being found between two conical hills where there are fountains from which half of the water flows northward to Egypt and the other half to Ethiopia. King Psammetichus had these measured with a sounding line and found that there was no bottom to these fountains.

The land rises beyond Elephantine, and oxen are used to drag the boats upriver for four days until a smooth plain is reached where the Nile flows around an island called Tachompso. Above the island is a huge lake, where you disembark and travel for forty days overland, as the river is full of sharp peaks and too dangerous for a boat. Now you can continue by boat for eight days to reach a great city called Meroe, which is the capital of the Ethiopians. Further travel over the same amount of time which passed since you left Elephantine brings you to the land of the Deserters: these consist of the descendants of two hundred and forty thousand soldiers who abandoned their posts in the time of King Psammetichus. The King had not relieved the garrisons for three years, and the troops abandoned their wives and children and were given lands to occupy by the King of Ethiopia in exchange for certain services rendered.

More information comes from Libyans who travelled for many days over their desert before coming across trees and were taken to a city of a people of very short stature and black complexion which had a great river flowing through it leading out of Libya to join the Nile.

Egyptians who worship Zeus offer only goats in sacrifice, whereas those who worship Dionysius sacrifice sheep instead. The Egyptians worship Heracles, who is one of the twelve gods, but this Heracles seems different from the one which is familiar to the Greeks. The Egyptians maintain that, seventeen thousand years before the reign of Amasis, their eight gods became twelve and another of these gods is Pan, represented, just as he is in Greece, with the face and legs of a goat.

The pig is regarded as unclean, and if a man accidently touches a pig, he instantly rushes to the river and plunges in with all his clothes on to wash himself. Swineherds are not allowed into the temples, and must intermarry amongst themselves. Pigs are sacrificed only to Dionysius and to the Moon for reasons of which I am acquainted but prefer not to mention. Dionysian festivals are celebrated just as in Greece, except for the fact that the Egyptians have no choral dances. Melampus, the son of Amytheon, introduced these customs and ceremonies to Greece, for it cannot be a coincidence that the Greek ceremonies so closely resemble those of Egypt.

With the exception of Poseidon, Hera, Hestia, Themis, the Graces, the Nereids and the Dioscuri, all other gods familiar to the Greeks have been known from time immemorial in Egypt. I believe that the Greeks obtained their knowledge of the other gods from the Pelasgi and of Poseidon from the Libyans. The Egyptians differ from the Greeks in extending no divine honours to heroes. The Egyptians were the first to introduce solemn assemblies, processions and litanies to the gods, all of which are recent practices in Greece but established in Egypt from antiquity. The most important assembly is in honour of Artemis, held in the city of Busiris, followed by others, to Isis (Demeter) and Athena, and to the Sun and Ares. Many thousands of men and women assemble for these festivals, each of which has its own character and customs.

There are many domestic animals in Egypt, but it is curious how they behave toward cats. Kittens are seized and taken off and killed, and if a cat suffers a natural death in a private house, the inhabitants shave off their eyebrows. If a dog dies, they shave the head and the whole of the body. Dead cats are taken to the city of Bubastis, where they are embalmed and stored in sacred repositories. Similarly, Ibises are conveyed to Heliopolis and shrew-mice to the city of Buto.

Crocodiles are esteemed sacred by some Egyptians and treated as an enemy by others. Those who hunt crocodiles bait a hook with some pork, which they cause to be carried to the middle of the river and then hold a living pig on the bank so that the crocodile hears its cries and makes its way toward the sound but encounters the bait along the way. They haul the crocodile to the land and cover its eyes with mud, after which it is easy to slay. The Hippopotamus is regarded as sacred, as are Otters found in the Nile. Of all the fish, only the lepidotus and the eel are venerated. They also revere some birds, including the Phoenix, of which they tell an incredible story in which the bird, which is similar to an eagle in size, brings its parent, all plastered with myrrh, and buries it in the temple of the sun.

(Herodotus has much more here on Egypt.)

CAMBYSES

Cambyses, the son of Cyrus, forged an expedition against the Egyptians, who were ruled by their King, Amasis. The way it came about was that an Egyptian eye doctor, who had been sent to the Persian court at the request of Cyrus and who held a grudge against his countrymen, advised Cambyses to ask for the daughter of Amasis in marriage, for if he complied it might cause him discomfort and if he declined it might make Cambyses his enemy.

Amasis dreaded the power of the Persians and knew that Cambyses did not intend to make his daughter his wife, but to have her as a concubine. So he sent the last surviving daughter of the late King Apries, named Nitetis, who was very beautiful and whom he decked out royally in gold and costly garments. Sometime later, when Cambyses was embracing Nitetis, he called her by her father's name whereupon she said to him: 'O King, thou knowest not that thou hast been cheated by Amasis, for I am the daughter of Apries, who was the lord and master of Amasis until he rebelled against him and had him put to death'. So Cambyses quarrelled with Amasis and brought his army into Egypt.

CONQUEST OF EGYPT

We should note that the Egyptians claim that Cambyses was, in fact, himself the son of Cyrus and Nitetis, but I doubt this story, as the Persians would not have allowed a bastard to reign if there had been a legitimate heir. Cambyses is the son of Cassandané, an Achaemenian and not an Egyptian.

Another story I have heard was that a Persian lady came to visit the wives of Cyrus and praised the beautiful children of Cassandané, whereupon she expressed her vexations that Cyrus' thoughts were now only for his new concubine from Egypt. Cambyses, who was just ten years old, swore to his mother that he would turn Egypt upside down for her, and that was the origin of the quarrel.

Another significant event was the escape of Phanes, a Halicarnassian, from Egypt to the court of Cambyses. Phanes, a mercenary of no small account, was able to tell Cambyses the military secrets of Amasis and advised him how to cross the desert and ask for safe passage from the King of the Arabs. This passage involves crossing a desert for three days with no water, as the custom of using earthen jars stored at Memphis had not yet begun. The Arabs had sworn friendship to Cambyses in front of his messengers by making a cut with a sharp stone on the inside of each hand, and then moistening each of seven stones with blood while calling upon their gods Dionysius and Urania. The Arabs then filled as many skins as they could with water and transported them into the desert by camel to await the arrival of the Persian army.

Amasis died after a forty-four year reign during which no great misfortune had befallen him, and his son, Psammenitus, commanded the Egyptian army waiting for Cambyses at the mouth of the Nile. A strange omen had occurred, in that rain had fallen for the very first time in the Egyptian city of Thebes.

Many of the mercenaries in the Egyptian army were Greeks and Carians who were angry with Phanes for bringing a foreign army into Egypt. They found a way to take revenge upon him by leading his sons, whom he had left behind in Egypt, out in front of the eyes of their father and slaying them one by one over a vessel into which they poured water and wine so that all the soldiers could taste the blood before they went into battle. The subsequent fight was stubborn, with vast numbers slain on both sides, until the Egyptians finally turned and fled.

I can relate a wonderful thing which the natives pointed out to me when I visited the battlefield. The skulls of the Persians break easily when you strike one with a pebble but the Egyptian skulls are so strong that you cannot break them even with a large stone. The reason they gave me was that Egyptians have shaven heads from childhood and the action of the sun makes the skull thick and hard and also prevents baldness, whereas the Persians wear turbans and shield their heads in shadow, with their skulls rendered feeble as a consequence.

MEMPHIS

The Egyptians fled to Memphis, and Cambyses sent a ship to sail up the Nile to invite them to surrender, but crowds poured forth from the city and destroyed the ship and tore the limbs from the ship's crew. As a result, Memphis was besieged and, in due course, surrendered to Cambyses. The Libyans also gave themselves up to Cambyses without a battle and agreed to pay tribute to him. The Cyrenaeans and the Barcaeans followed suit and sent tribute, but Cambyses was angry that they had sent no more than five hundred minea of gold and snatched the money and scattered it amongst his soldiers.

Ten days after the fall of Memphis, Cambyses set out to try the spirit of Psammenitus, whom he held prisoner. Firstly, he ordered his daughter, together with the daughters of the other nobles, to dress as slaves and parade in front of their fathers with a pitcher to draw water. All of the fathers, save Psammenitus, shed tears and uttered cries of woe. Next, he roped together two thousand Egyptians, amongst whom were the sons of Psammenitus, and had them put to death as punishment for the killing of the crew of his ship. Again, Psammenitus showed no signs of grief, but, when he espied one of his friends reduced to begging and asking alms of the soldiers, Psammenitus burst into tears and smote himself on the head. This was reported to Cambyses who demanded an explanation from Psammenitus: 'O son of Cyrus, my own troubles were too great for tears but the woes of my friend deserved them, for when a man falls from splendour to beggary in his old age, one may well weep for him'. Many of the Persians, and also Croesus, who had come to Egypt with Cambyses, wept, and Cambyses thought the explanation just and spared Psammenitus his life and also that of his son, although the messengers were too late to save the son.

PSAMMENITUS

Cambyses had Psammenitus live with him and gave him no more harsh treatment, and Psammenitus might have had Egypt returned to him as governor, for the Persians often treat the sons of kings with honour and even give them their father's kingdoms to them to govern. However, he was discovered stirring revolt, and Cambyses compelled him to drink bulls' blood, which presently caused his death.

Cambyses now left Memphis for Sais and entered the palace of Amasis and ordered the embalmed corpse of the King brought to him, upon which it was subjected to insult by being pricked with goads and having the hair plucked from it. The body had been embalmed, however, and refused to come apart, so Cambyses bade them burn it, which is an unlawful practice amongst both the Egyptians and the Persians. The Persians hold fire to be a god, and the Egyptians believe it to be a wild animal which eats whatever it can seize and then dies with the matter it feeds upon. The Egyptians claim that Amasis had been warned of this fate by an oracle and had buried a second body in the tomb which received these insults.

Cambyses now took counsel and planned three expeditions against the Carthaginians, the Ammonians, and the Ethiopians. He sent his spies forth and ordered his fleet to sail against Carthage, but the Phoenicians refused to go, as they were bound to the Carthaginians by solemn oaths and thought it wicked to make war upon their own children. Cambyses thought it right not to force war upon the Phoenicians, as they had yielded themselves to the Persians and all of his sea service depended on them. So the Carthaginians escaped servitude.

ETHIOPIA

The spies dispatched to Ethiopia had taken gifts of a purple robe, a golden neck chain and amulets, a box of myrrh, and a cask of palm wine. The Ethiopians are thought to be the tallest and handsomest men in the whole world and said to choose the tallest and strongest amongst them as their King.

The Ethiopian King knew that the messengers had been sent as spies and gave them a bow and bade them tell Cambyses to bring his army only when it had men of sufficient strength to pull this bow easily. He then took the purple robe and asked about its origin and, on hearing that the garment had been dyed, he discarded it as deceitful. He laughed at the neck chain and amulets, thinking them fetters as the Ethiopians had much stronger chains. He said the same about the myrrh as he had about the robe but he was greatly delighted with the wine, whereupon he asked what the Persian King liked to eat and how long-lived were the Persians. His people lived to one hundred and twenty, he claimed, and ate only boiled meat and drank nothing but milk. He showed them a fountain where the water was so weak that nothing would float in it, neither wood nor any lighter substance, and implied that their constant use of this water must be what makes them so long-lived. The messengers were also allowed to behold crystal coffins containing corpses that could be seen through transparent walls.

The spies returned to Cambyses, who was so enraged at the reply from the Ethiopian King that he set out immediately with the Persian part of his army, without provisions, leaving the Greeks behind. When he reached Thebes, he dispatched some fifty thousand men with orders to subdue the Ammonians and he went on against the Ethiopians. After the army had got but a fifth of the way, they were forced to eat their beasts, but still Cambyses marched on. When finally they reached the desert and had no means of sustenance, the soldiers cast lots for one man out of every ten who was to be slain for food for the others. Only then was Cambyses alarmed and began a retreat, having lost large numbers of his men. He returned to Memphis and dismissed the Greek part of his army, and thus ended the attack on Ethiopia.

The army dispatched to attack the Ammonians had to march seven days across the desert to a town called Oasis and soon afterwards, as they settled down for a midday meal, after completing about half the journey, a wind from the south came up and whipped up columns of sand which covered the troops, and the whole army disappeared.

APIS

Around the time at which Cambyses arrived at Memphis, the god Apis appeared to the Egyptians and the townspeople put on their gayest garments and began feasting and celebrating. Cambyses took this as an insult and thought that they were celebrating the misfortune of his armies and condemned them all to suffer death. He then ordered the priests to bring Apis to him and they returned with a calf with the following marks – black in colour with a square spot of white on his forehead, the figure of an eagle on his back, double hairs in his tail and a beetle upon his tongue. Cambyses drew his dagger and aimed at the belly of the animal but missed his mark and stabbed it in the thigh. He then scourged the priests and forbade any Egyptians from keeping the festival on pain of death.

The Egyptians say that Cambyses was smitten with madness for this crime. His first outrage was to have his brother Smerdis slain, for Smerdis had been the only one of the Persians able to draw the Ethiopian bow and Cambyses had a dream in which a messenger had come from Persia with tidings that Smerdis sat on the throne.

Next, he slew his sister with whom he had fallen in love and taken as his wife. Cambyses had consulted the judges who administered the law in Persia, and they had answered him that 'whereas there is no law in Persia allowing a brother to marry his sister, we have found a law that the King of Persia can do as he pleases'.

Soon afterwards, he also took a second sister as a wife and she suffered death at his hands in the following manner. Cambyses had set a young dog to fight the cub of a lioness and the dog was getting the worst of it when a puppy from the same litter broke free and came to its aid and they together fought and conquered the lion. This pleased Cambyses, but his sister wept and when Cambyses asked her what the matter was, she said this made her think of Smerdis and how no one had come to his aid, and for this she was put to death. Another version is that his sister was eating a lettuce and seeing the lettuce stripped of its leaves began to weep. 'Why are you weeping?' asked Cambyses. 'Because you have stripped the House of Cyrus bare', she replied. Cambyses beat her in a rage, and she miscarried and died.

Cambyses asked his court whether he was greater than his father and received the reply that, of course, he was, for he held dominion over all the lands conquered by his father and Egypt also and the sea. Croesus spoke and said: 'In my judgement, O son of Cyrus, thou are not equal to thy father because thou hast not yet left behind such a son as he', which pleased Cambyses greatly. Prexaspes, the most loyal of the Persians, whom Cambyses had entrusted with the murder of his brother, when asked what the Persians thought of their King, answered that the Persians praise Cambyses for all his qualities apart from his love of wine. Cambyses took offense and to prove to Prexaspes that the Persians had no grounds for that remark he said: 'Look at your son standing over there. If I can draw this bow and shoot him in the heart then I must be sober. If not then I will allow that the Persians are right', upon which he drew the bow and shot the boy, who was his cupbearer, dead. The boy's chest was cut open and the arrow found to have pierced his heart. 'O Lord, I doubt even that God could shoot so dexterously', said Prexaspes fearing for his own life.

Cambyses committed many more outrages while he was in Memphis, upon both the Persians and their allies. He mocked the Egyptian holy rites and temples and entered the temple of the Cabiri and made sport of the images and even burnt them. Cambyses also had twelve of the greatest Persian nobles put to death without charge by burying them up to their necks in the earth. Croesus warned Cambyses that he would incite revolt if he carried on behaving in this manner, but Cambyses took up his bow and tried to slay him, although he managed to run away. Cambyses ordered Croesus put to death, but his servants thought that he might change his mind and decided to keep him alive for the time being and let Cambyses know in the course of time that Croesus was still alive. 'I am glad of it', exclaimed Cambyses, but had the servants put to death for disobeying his orders.

POLYCRATES

Polycrates had led an insurrection and become master of the island of Samos together with his two brothers, Pantagnotus and Syloson. They had divided the island into thirds, but Polycrates killed the former and banished the latter, making himself master of the whole island. Polycrates built up a navy of a hundred pentenconters and a thousand archers and plundered without distinction, for he felt that a friend would be better pleased if you gave back what you had plundered from him than if you spared him at first.

The Egyptian King Amasis had an allegiance with Polycrates but wrote to him after observing his many successes and pointed out that no man could expect to have only good fortune and that a calamity must be expected soon. Perhaps Polycrates should look through his treasury and select an item that he held dear and throw it away lest a worse calamity befell him. Polycrates took this advice and took his favourite golden ring with an emerald stone and threw it into the sea. Now, a fisherman in the area caught a very large and beautiful fish and decided to present it to Polycrates, who was so pleased that he invited the fisherman to dine with him. The servants began to prepare the meal and were surprised to find the ring in the belly of the fish and so it was returned to the tyrant. When Amasis heard of this, he withdrew his alliance, for he thought a great misfortune must be imminent and did not wish to share the suffering of his ally.

Cambyses had requested help from Polycrates when he set forth on his expedition to Egypt, and Polycrates had selected those Samians he thought most likely to revolt and sent them in forty ships to Cambyses with a message that Cambyses could deploy them as he liked but that they were not expected to return. These same Samians managed to return and better Polycrates in a naval battle, but they were too few to conquer his forces and they set sail to ask the Lacedaemonians for help. They gave a great and heartfelt speech, but at its conclusion the Spartans said that the speech was so long that they had forgotten the first half of it and then could not make head nor tail of the second half. The Samians tried again the next day, but this time they brought forth an empty bag and simply said: 'this bag needs flour'. The Spartans understood and offered help, as they were already displeased with their countrymen, who had previously seized a silver bowl they had sent to the Persian King and, together with the Corinthians, they set off for Samos.

They besieged Samos for forty days and would have taken the city but for Polycrates leading a charge in person. This was Sparta's first expedition into Asia, but after making no progress, they decided to return to the Peloponnese, although there is a story that Polycrates paid them off with coins made of lead but coated with gold. The Samians had requested help from the Dorians. They set sail and landed on the island of Siphnos, which was very rich at the time, and asked the inhabitants to lend them ten talents. The people of Siphnos, however, had heard, from an oracle, of their coming in their vermillion ships and refused, after which the Samians began to plunder the island and had to be bought off with one hundred talents. The Samians used this money to buy the island of Hydrea and then went on to found the city of Cydonia in Crete, which flourished for five years. However, they were attacked by the Eginetans and enslaved on account of an ancient grudge which the Eginetans bore against Samos.

Three of the greatest works in Greece are to be found in Samos. Eupalinus the architect was responsible for building a tunnel seven furlongs long and eight feet wide all the way through a hill one hundred and fifty fathoms high, with a second, adjacent, channel which brought water through pipes from an abundant source into the city. They also have a mole twenty fathoms deep and two furlongs long all around the harbour and the most imposing temple in all of Greece, built by Rhoecus, a Samian architect.

DARIUS

Cambyses lingered in Egypt, still losing his senses, and two Magi took advantage of the fact that the murder of Smerdis had been carried out in secret and put their own brother onto the Persian throne, as he was also called Smerdis and bore some resemblance to the son of Cyrus. They sent out messengers throughout the empire to announce that Smerdis now controlled the empire and so Cambyses came to hear of this.

Cambyses realised that the dream he had which had caused him to have Smerdis killed, was in fact about the brother of the Magi and he was greatly grieved that he had needlessly killed his own brother. He immediately gathered his army and set off for Persia. One day, as he jumped onto his horse, the sheath of his sword fell off and he stabbed himself in the thigh in exactly the same place that he had wounded the god Apis. This happened in a place called Agbatana in Syria, and he remembered an oracle that said that he would die in Agbatana, although he had thought it to be the Medean Agbatana, where the royal treasury of the Persians was situated and not Agbatana in Syria.

Cambyses realised that he was doomed, and, after twenty days, by which time his wound had become gangrenous, he came to his senses and gathered his nobles together to tell them of how, in his folly, he had put his brother to death. 'So Smerdis, the son of Cyrus, is lost to you' he said 'and this usurper is the brother of the Magi who wield royal power back at court. I urge you all, and those of Persian blood in particular, to recover this power that has been taken by fraud and put a Persian and not a Mede back on the throne'. Soon afterwards, Cambyses died, having reigned for seven years and five months and leaving no children. Everyone was convinced that the

Smerdis on the throne was actually his brother and that Cambyses had spoken out of madness, for Prexaspes had to deny that he had slain Smerdis, as it was not safe for him to admit that a son of Cyrus had met death at his hands.

SMERDIS THE IMPOSTER

The Magus called Smerdis dispensed great benefits to all, with the exception of the Persians, in that he exempted every nation under his rule from war service and from taxes for a period of three years. After eight months, a Persian noble named Otanes became suspicious because Smerdis never left the palace and had never been seen by any of the Persian nobility. He asked his daughter, who had been married to Cambyses and thus was now married to Smerdis, whether the King was indeed the son of Cyrus. She could not answer, and when Otanes further discovered that Atossa, the sister of Cambyses, had not set sight on Smerdis, his suspicion grew.

Now Smerdis the Magian had had his ears cut off for a heinous crime in the lifetime of Cyrus, and so Otanes bid his daughter wait for Smerdis to sleep and then feel his head to see if he had ears. She did this stealthily when her turn came to sleep with the Magus and she reported to her father that, indeed, the King had no ears.

Otanes gathered seven nobles in the greatest confidence and told them of his discovery. They were Intaphernes, Gobryas, Megabyzus, Aspathines, Hydarnes, and, finally, Darius, the youngest, and the son of Hystaspes, the governor of Susa. Darius urged them all to act without delay, warning that, if a single day passed without their doing so, he would himself go to Smerdis and denounce them all. They conceived a plan by which

Darius, who had just arrived from Susa, would deliver a message to the King accompanied by the other nobles, and their combined rank should suffice to get them into the presence of the imposter. After some debate they all agreed to act without delay.

Meanwhile, the Magus had befriended Prexaspes and offered him great gifts if he would once more declare that this Smerdis was truly the brother of Cambyses. Prexaspes agreed and addressed a crowd from atop a tower but, instead of confirming Smerdis in his position, he explained how he had murdered the real Smerdis on the orders of Cambyses and urged the Persians to reclaim the throne, before throwing himself from the tower to his death.

SEVEN CONSPIRATORS

The seven Persians were approaching the palace when they heard of the actions of Prexaspes, and some of the party, led by Otanes, were for delaying their action, whereas the others, led by Darius, were for pressing on. Just then they saw two pairs of vultures pursued and attacked by five pairs of hawks and they saw that they must continue. Everything went as planned until they came to the chamber of the King, who was discussing with another Magus what to do in the wake of Prexaspes' speech. The seven were forced to draw their daggers and overpower the guards and enter the chamber, where a fight ensued.

One Magus grabbed a spear and succeeded in striking Aspathines in the thigh and Intaphernes in the eye. At one point, Gobryas had the Magus in his grip and Darius could not strike because it was dark and he was fearful of smiting the Persian, but Gobryas urged him to strike them both down if necessary, and by good fortune the Magus was killed and Gobryas unharmed. The seven ran from the palace holding high the heads of the Magi and shouting to all, exclaiming what they had done.

The Persians now understood the fraud of the Magi and set about killing all the Magi they could find, and the remainder were spared only because night fell. This event is now celebrated by a festival called Magophonia, a day on which any Magus is wise to stay at home.

After five days had passed, the conspirators held a meeting to decide what to do, given the state of affairs. Otanes argued for the nation to decide its own affairs without the need for a King. 'Do not forget how Cambyses behaved in his tyranny and the haughtiness of the Magi. How can monarchy be a good thing when it allows a man to do whatever he likes? To my mind giving a person absolute power raises two evils in him: pride and envy. Together these lead to great wickedness. Now it seems strange that a King, who can do anything he likes, is subject to envy, but you can see envy in how they behave toward their citizens, for they become jealous of the most virtuous of citizens and have them put to death and listen to the most base of slanderers. A King is inconsistent and, if you give a King too much praise, he accuses you of fawning, and yet if you do not, he is offended because you do not show him enough respect. Worst of all is that they ignore the law of the land, putting people to death as they like and subjecting women to violence. I vote, therefore, that we do away with the monarchy and raise the people to power, for the people are all'.

Megabyzus then spoke out in favour of an oligarchy: 'I agree with Otanes, but calling the people to power does not seem to be the best advice, for we are just exchanging tyranny for the power of the mob. A tyrant at least knows what he is about, but a mob is rude and untaught and rushes into affairs like a stream swollen with rain. Let other nations be ruled by democracies while we Persians choose a certain number of our worthiest citizens and let them rule together, for thus it is likely that the best counsels will prevail'.

Lastly, Darius came forward: 'All that Megabyzus said against democracy was well said, but I maintain that a monarchy is better than both democracy and oligarchy. What government can be better than the counsel of the best man in the whole state? For a monarch governs a people who love him and keeps his measures against evildoers more secret than in other states. Oligarchies lead to struggles, as powerful men vie with each other, each wishing to become leader, and the system breaks down, eventually leading to monarchy. Democracies break down, not because of enmities, but because of the fact that close friendships create a group which champions its own affairs over the interests of others, and this is, eventually, challenged by a champion who is admired by all, again leading to monarchy. So both systems lead to monarchy, and let us not forget our current freedoms, which were arrived at through monarchy. Just as the rule of a single man recovered our freedom from slavery, my view is that we should keep to the rule of one'.

So the four remaining Persians voted in favour of the monarchy, and Otanes rose: 'Brother conspirators, it is plain that the King should be chosen by lot from amongst ourselves but I have no desire to be King and withdraw on condition that none of you shall claim to rule over me or my family for the generations to come'. So even today the family of Otanes is not bound to submit to the rule of the King, although they must obey the laws of the land. The six then took counsel and agreed that they would ride out the next morning beyond the city gates and that he whose horse neighed first after the sun came up would become King. The others would be free to enter the palace unannounced, unless the King was with one of his wives, and the King was bound to marry into one of their families.

DARIUS

Darius had a sharp-witted groom called Oebares and explained to him how the King was to be chosen and asked him, if he had any cleverness, to contrive a plan for the prize to fall to Darius. 'Master,' he replied,f 'set your mind at ease, for I know a charm that is sure not to fail', and Oebares took Darius' horse and his favourite mare and took them out into a suburb as soon as night fell. He tethered the mare and led the horse round and round several times before letting them come together.

The next day the six Persians met together just before dawn and exited through the city gates and began to ride around the city walls. As they came to the spot where the mare had been tethered the night before, the horse that Darius was riding sprang forward and neighed and just at that moment, even though the sky was clear, there was a bolt of lightning and a clap of thunder. Immediately, five Persians jumped off their horses and knelt down to their new King - Darius the King of the Persians.

Thus, Darius became King and all the peoples of Asia were subject to him, for Cyrus and then Cambyses had brought them all under, save the Arabians who had a league of friendship with the Persians, forged when they helped Cambyses into Egypt. Darius married in accordance with the customs of the Persians: two daughters of Cyrus, Atossa, who had been married to Cambyses and the Magus, and Artystone, a virgin, and also Parmys, the daughter of Smerdis and the son of

Cyrus, and the daughter of Otanes. Soon his power was established throughout the kingdom, and his first act as King was to have a stone carving inscribed: 'Darius, son of Hystaspes, by aid of his good horse and his good groom, Oebares, acquired the kingdom of the Persians'.

THE PERSIAN EMPIRE

Darius proceeded to establish twenty satrapies, and this divided the empire into governments responsible for paying taxes. The taxes were paid in Babylonian talents for silver and Euboic Minae for gold, there being seventy Minae for each Babylonian talent. Darius became known as a huckster, as it seemed to the Persians that he was obsessed with gold, whereas Cambyses was considered a master of slaves and Cyrus a father.

The twenty satrapies covered many nations: the first consisted of the Ionians, Magnesians, Aeolians, Carians, Lycians, Milyans and the Pamphylians, who paid a fixed tribute of four hundred talents of silver. The Mysians, Lydians, Lasonians, Cabalians and Hygennians paid five hundred talents. The right-hand coast of the Hellespontians, the Phrygians, Asiatic Thracians, Paphlagonians, Mariandynians and Syrians paid three hundred and sixty talents. The fourth satrapy was accounted for by the Cilicians, who gave three hundred and sixty white horses and five hundred talents of silver, of which one hundred and forty went to paying the cavalry required to guard the country. The area from the city of Posideium, containing Phoenicia, Palestine Syria and Cyprus, with the exception of the districts belonging to Arabia, which were free of tax, paid three hundred and fifty talents. The Egyptian satrapy, including parts of Libya paid seven hundred talents, not including the fisheries of Lake Moeris or the corn supplied to the 120,000 Persian troops at Memphis. The seventh satrapy, consisting of the Gandarians, the Dadicae and the Aparytae, paid tribute of one hundred and seventy talents. Susa and the other parts of Cissia paid three hundred talents. Babylonia and the rest of Assyria paid one thousand talents of silver and five hundred boy eunuchs. Media, including Agbatana, together with the Paricanians and Orthocorybantes, paid four hundred and sixty talents. The Caspians, Pausicae, Pantimathi and Daritae formed the eleventh satrapy, paying two hundred talents. The Bactrian tribes as far as the Aegli paid three hundred and sixty talents. Four hundred talents were paid by the thirteenth satrapy, containing the countries from Pactyica and Armenia reaching to the Euxine. The Sagartians, Sarangians, Thamanaeans, Utians and Mycians and the inhabitants of the Erythraean Sea islands paid six hundred talents and also received those whom the King banished. The Sacans and Caspians gave two hundred and fifty talents. The Parthians, Chorasmians, Sogdians, and Arians gave six hundred talents. The Paricanians and Ethiopians of Asia gave four hundred talents. The Matienians, Saspeires, and Alarodians paid two hundred talents. The Moschi, Tibareni, Macrones, Mosynoeci and Mares had to pay three hundred talents. Finally, the Indians, who were more numerous than any other nation, paid three hundred and sixty talents of gold dust and formed the twentieth satrapy.

In the Euboic scale, this comes to nine thousand, five hundred and forty talents in total, and, if gold is worth thirteen times the value of silver, Indian gold dust is worth four thousand, three hundred and eighty talents. Thus Darius received fourteen thousand, five hundred and sixty talents each year, which he had melted down and run into earthen vessels from which he could make coins as required. Later this was increased with the tribute from the Aegean Islands and from Thessaly, and only the country of the Persians is altogether free of tax.

Some nations had no fixed amount of tribute but brought gifts regularly to the King. The Ethiopians bordering Egypt brought two choenices of gold, two hundred logs of ebony, five boys, and twenty elephant tusks. The Colchians every fifth year brought one hundred boys and one hundred maidens, and the Arabs brought every year one thousand talents of frankincense.

INDIA

The Indian people are numerous and have many different tribes, some of whom are wanderers, and one tribe, the Padaeans, lives in the marshes alongside the rivers, living off raw fish. If one of them, male or female, falls sick, their friends kill them, despite all of their protestations, and feast on their body, and if they manage to reach old age they are then offered in sacrifice to their gods and afterwards eaten. Another tribe refuses to eat any meat and has no dwelling houses and if one of them becomes sick he goes off into the wilderness and lies down to die, and nobody has any concern for the sick or the dead.

I have observed that in India the animals and birds are much bigger than those found elsewhere, excepting the horses. Gold is found in huge quantities, and there are trees that produce a fruit containing a wool as good as that of sheep. One tribe living near the city of Caspatyrus is more warlike, and the men go out to collect gold which is found in the desert sand. Here live some large sand ants, larger than a fox and smaller than a dog, who burrow into the sand, throwing up great heaps of it which contain gold. The Indians go to collect the gold with camels, always taking three camels: two males strapped together, with a female who has just dropped her young, in the middle. The men ride on the female and drench themselves with water, for they must go and collect the gold in the hottest part of the day when the sand ants are least active. They rush and fill their bags with sand while the ants begin to muster and then depart at full speed with the ants in pursuit. This is why they take care to have a female camel who wants to rush home to her young, to make sure that they have the speed to avoid a dispute with the ants.

ARABIA

Arabia is the southernmost part of the empire and the only country to produce frankincense, myrrh, cassia, cinnamon and ladanum. The trees that produce the gum from which frankincense is made are guarded by winged serpents whose numbers must be kept in check. Indeed, I have observed that timid animals which constitute prey to others produce young in abundance, so that the species may not be entirely eaten up and lost, but that savage creatures are made unfruitful. Thus, the hare is continually producing young but a lion brings forth young but once in her lifetime, because, as soon as the cub is about to be born, it scratches and causes damage inside her, so she cannot have a second litter. Now if these winged serpents could increase as much as their nature would allow, it would be impossible for man to maintain himself upon the earth, but it happens that, as they mate, the female seizes the male by the neck and bites right through, although the young repay the debt by gnawing through their mother in an effort to be born.

No one knows where cinnamon grows, but great birds gather it into their nests in a certain part of Arabia. Their nests cannot be reached because they are made of mud and designed to cling to the sheer face of a cliff which cannot be climbed by man or any other beast. The Arabs have a cunning practice by which they cut up all of the oxen and asses that die and place the meat on the ground near these nests, whereupon the great birds swoop down and take the meat into their nests. The weight is often so substantial that the nest collapses and falls to the ground, allowing the Arabs to come and collect the cinnamon which has fallen along with the nest.

Ladanum is produced in an even stranger fashion, as it is gathered from the beards of he-goats, where it is found sticking like a gum, having been rubbed off from the bushes that they graze upon. Arabia is full of spices, and the air there is sweet with the smell of them, but there is also an interesting kind of sheep with a tail three cubits long. The tail is so long that the shepherds have to make little trucks out of wood for each sheep, so that the tail does not drag along the ground and become bruised and covered in sores.

The last inhabited land toward the south is Ethiopia, where one may observe plenty of gold, huge elephants and all sorts of trees, including ebony, and the people are taller and more handsome than anywhere else.

EUROPE

I am unsure about the extreme western parts of Europe, for I cannot confirm the existence of the river Eridanus, which empties into the northern sea where amber is produced. Nor can I verify the existence of the tin islands called the Cassiterides. Nevertheless, tin and amber do certainly come to us from the ends of the earth. The northern parts of Europe are also rich in gold, and the story is that one-eyed men steal it from griffins, but, again, I cannot believe that there are one-eyed men who otherwise resemble the rest of mankind.

There is a plain in Asia which is shut in on all sides by a mountain range with five passes, and a mighty river called the Aces flows there. Once the Persians conquered this land and they shut off the five openings, and the river flooded into the plain, creating a great sea. The five nations who formerly used the waters now had no source of irrigation for their crops in the summer and were forced to petition the Great King. The King would open the sluice gates to the nation which had the greatest need of the water but never until he had received a large sum of money over and above the normal tribute.

OROETES

Around the time of the last sickness of Cambyses, Mitrobates, the ruler of the satrapy of Dascyleium, was talking with Oroetes, the governor of Sardis, and said to him: 'Oroetes. Are you worthy to be called a man when a common citizen with the help of fifteen men at arms has mastered Samos and remains King when Samos lies near to your government and you have omitted to bring it under the dominion of your King?', causing Oroetes to desire the destruction of Polycrates.

Now Polycrates was the first man to conceive of having an empire of the sea, perhaps with the exception of King Minos of Knossos, and he desired to rule over the whole of Ionia. Oroetes knew this and sent him a message: 'Oroetes knows of the desires of Polycrates and sees that you have not the means to achieve them and offers a plan to serve yourself and preserve me, for King Cambyses is bent on my destruction. Come and fetch me away and share my wealth and make yourself master of Greece, and if you doubt my word then send a trusted follower to see my treasury'. So Polycrates sent Maeandrius, who was shown the treasures of Oroetes, after the latter had filled a large number of boxes with stones and placed a layer of gold coins on top.

Polycrates now prepared to set sail, although his friends and soothsayers warned him not to go. His daughter dreamt that she saw her father suspended in the air, washed by Jove and anointed by the sun, and begged him not to depart. Polycrates would not listen and threatened to keep her unmarried for many years if he returned in safety. 'Better to remain unmarried for many years than lose a father', she entreated, but Polycrates set sail for Magnesia and Oroetes.

Oroetes slew Polycrates in a manner most unworthy of his rank and lofty ambition, for only the tyrants of Syracuse can be compared with Polycrates for magnificence, and hung him on a cross. He spared the rest of the Samian crew, which included many friends of Polycrates, and also Democedes, who was the best physician then living.

After the death of King Cambyses, Oroetes had not helped the Persians who had been robbed of the throne by the Magus and, indeed, he caused the death of Mitrobates and his son, who both held the highest rank amongst the Persians. Oroetes continued to cause trouble once Darius was on the throne, and Darius was at a loss for how to deal with him, as his foe had a thousand bodyguards and open warfare was impossible, given the unpredictable state of the kingdom.

Darius asked for help, and lots were drawn and the task fell to Bagaeus who conceived and executed the following plan. He prepared a number of letters, all sealed with the King's signet, and departed for Sardis, where he was brought into the presence of Oroetes. He uncovered the letters one by one and commanded the King's secretary to read them out. Once he had seen that the court respected the word of the King, he passed over a letter that instructed the guards to stop guarding Oroetes and he saw them stand down. He then handed over the last letter which ordered the guards to kill Oroetes. So did retribution for the death of Polycrates overtake Oroetes, and his treasures were forfeited to the King.

DEMOCEDES

Soon afterwards, Darius badly sprained his ankle while dismounting from a horse, and his Egyptian physicians made the problem worse, causing him great pain. After seven days and nights in pain and without sleep, Darius sent for Democedes, who had been enslaved by Oroetes together with the other Samians who had accompanied Polycrates. Democedes denied that he was a physician, as he feared that he would never be allowed home to Crotona again. Darius saw through this and brought out physicians' tools, and Democedes thus managed firstly to get the King to sleep and then cured his ankle. Darius had thought that he might lose the use of his foot and was so pleased that he presented Democedes with two sets of fetters made of gold, whereupon Democedes asked if Darius wanted to double his suffering because he had brought him back to health? Darius was pleased and bade his eunuchs present Democedes to his wives, each of whom bestowed gifts of gold on the physician.

Now that Democedes had cured Darius, he held the highest honour and dined at his table each day and was able to persuade Darius to spare the Egyptian physicians who had failed him and also to rescue an Elean soothsayer who had followed the fortunes of Polycrates.

Democedes, however, still pined for Greece. Atossa, the daughter of Cyrus who was also married to Darius, developed a cyst on her breast that she concealed for a while until the sore grew too big and so, at last, she sent for Democedes. He made her promise, firstly, that, if he was successful, she would grant him any wish, although he assured her it would be nothing to make her blush, and then cured her. Once she had heard his request, she spoke one night to Darius: 'My Lord, it seems strange to me that, with your mighty power, great wealth, and youth, you do not pursue some noble achievement for the Persians, so that they regard you as a man, and thus prevent idleness from creating any threat to your authority'. Darius replied: 'Dear lady, I have been thinking similar thoughts and plan to build a bridge which will join our continent with the other and then bring war to the Scythians'. Atossa replied: 'Lord, perhaps the war with Scythia can be delayed, for you can fight them at any time. I beg you to lead your host first into Greece for I desire a Lacedaemonian maid and also Argive, Athenian, and Corinthian women. Furthermore, there is already a man at court who can guide you: he who cured your foot'. Darius responded: 'Very well dear Lady, as you want me first to test the strength of the Greeks, I shall send forth spies, and once we have perfect knowledge of them, I can begin the war'.

Darius gathered fifteen nobles and asked them to accompany Democedes on his mission to Greece and not to let him run away and escape. He then asked Democedes to lead the mission and allowed him to take all his wealth as a gift to his fathers and brothers, and also contributed a merchant ship laden with treasures as a gift from the King. Democedes, suspecting guile on behalf of the King, said that he would leave his own treasures to enjoy on his return but would accept the ship as a gift from the King, and the party went down to Sidon in Phoenicia and took charge of two triremes and a merchant ship. They began to explore the coast of Greece until they reached Tarentum, in Italy, where King Aristophilides took pity on Democedes and detained the Persian ships as spies, leaving Democedes to escape to his home town of Crotona.

Soon, Aristophilides released the Persians, who sailed to Crotona in pursuit of Democedes and caught hold of him in the marketplace. Some of the Crotoniats were frightened of the Persian King and wanted to give Democedes up, but others prevailed and they seized the merchant ship and sent the Persians on their way. As they were leaving, Democedes begged them to tell Darius that he was betrothed to the daughter of Milo, a famous wrestler. The Persians were shipwrecked on the way home and held captive by the inhabitants of Iapygia until rescued by Gillus, who had been banished from Tarentine and paid their ransom from his own funds. Back at the Persian court, Darius thanked Gillus for rescuing the Persians and granted him any wish, whereupon he requested that Darius restore him to the Tarentines and end his banishment. The Cnidians could not, however, persuade the Tarentines and were too weak to pursue the matter by force, and that concludes the story of the way in which the first Persian spies entered Greece.

SYLOSON

Darius now besieged and took Samos, which was the first city that he conquered, and this is how it came about.

Many Greeks had flocked to the Persian army when Cambyses led his expedition into Egypt, and included amongst them was Syloson, the brother of Polycrates, who had been exiled from Samos. One day Syloson was wearing a red cloak and went to the market place at Memphis and came across Darius, who was then a bodyguard and of no great account. Darius desired the cloak and offered to buy it, upon which Syloson replied that no amount of money would induce him to part with the cloak, but that he would give it to Darius for nothing if he desired it so.

Luckily for Syloson, Darius eventually became the Great King of Persia and Syloson made his way to Susa, where he declared himself a benefactor of the King.

Darius was amazed that any Greek could claim to be his benefactor, for very few Greeks had been to his court since he had become King. Syloson was brought forward and the story told, upon which Darius offered him large amounts of gold and silver as a reward for his service. 'Give me not silver or gold', said Syloson, 'but restore me my land of Samos, now ruled over by a slave after Oroetes put my brother Polycrates to death, although I beg you restore it to me unharmed with no bloodshed or captivity'.

Maeandrius had been Polycrates' deputy and raised an altar to Jove, which you can still see. As soon as he heard of the death of Polycrates, he called the people together to announce that he had none of the ambition of Polycrates and had no desire to lord it over other men and would retire and leave the government to the people if they would pay him six talents and install him as the priest of the temple. The citizens, led by Telesarchus, abused him by asking him to account for the money he had already fingered and Maeandrius, as a result, decided to keep the kingdom for himself after all. He called each of the leading citizens in turn to view the accounts and imprisoned them, and soon afterwards, when Maeandrius was ill, his brother, Lycaretus, killed all the prisoners, thinking that Maeandrius was going to die and wishing to secure his own access to the throne.

The Persians arrived in Samos shortly thereafter, and Maeandrius, and Otanes, one of the seven conspirators, came to an agreement by which Maeandrius agreed to leave the island under certain terms, and so the Persians brought their thrones to the city and the matter seemed to be settled. However Charilaus, another brother of Maeandrius, had been languishing in jail and sought an audience with his brother: 'O meanest of men, how can you keep your own innocent brother in chains and not have the heart to take revenge on these Persians who drive you out, and render you a homeless wanderer from your lands. Lend me your soldiers to take your revenge, while you first slip away from the island'.

So it was that Maeandrius left with his riches and Charilaus took the mercenaries, set upon the unsuspecting Persians and attacked and killed many Persians of note who were going about in litters. After the initial surprise however, the rest of the Persian army took the citadel and Otanes saw what a calamity had taken place and ordered the slaughter of every man and boy. So the promise was not upheld and Syloson received the island stripped entirely of all its men, although, after some time, Otanes was induced to repopulate it, after a dream which he experienced during a serious illness.

Meanwhile, Maeandrius had arrived in Sparta to request help from Cleomenes, the son of King Anaxandridas. Once he saw the extent of the treasure that Maeandrius had brought with him, Cleomenes refused the gift and exhibited surpassing honesty and said to the elders that: 'it would be best if the Samian stranger were sent away from Sparta, for his riches are so great that he might bend some other Spartan to his aims'. Thus Maeandrius received notice that he must leave the city.

INTAPHERNES

One of the seven conspirators against the Magus lost his life soon after the outbreak, in the following manner.

Intaphernes had gone to visit the palace and had the right to enter it unannounced, as he was one of the seven. The guards, however, refused him entry on the grounds that the King was with his wife. Intaphernes refused to believe this and cut off their noses and ears and hung them around their necks.

Darius saw the mutilation done to the two guards and feared a conspiracy against him, so he called all of the remaining conspirators to see if they approved of the actions of Intaphernes. He found no wider conspiracy and so had Intaphernes and his children and kinsmen imprisoned and condemned to death.

Every day the wife of Intaphernes came to the palace gates, weeping and wailing, until Darius took pity on her: 'Lady, Darius offers you the life of one of your kinsmen; choose who you will of the prisoners that they may live'. 'Please Lord spare my brother', she cried after a little deliberation. 'Why do you choose your brother and not your husband or one of your children?' asked Darius and the lady replied: 'Sire, my mother and father are dead and I will never have another brother but I can marry again to have another husband and children'. So Darius spared her elder brother and the rest of the family of Intaphernes was put to death.

BABYLONIA REVOLTS

The Babylonians had profited during the time during which the Magus was King and had made every preparation for the siege and defence of Babylon. Each householder had chosen one woman, whichever he liked, having first set apart their mothers, and gathered the others in a public place and had them strangled so they would not be a burden on the stores of food. They now rebelled openly, and Darius was forced to march an army to the city gates, where he was taunted: 'Go back to your homes Persians, you will not take this city until mules foal'.

The army of Darius could not prevail even when he tried the same stratagem which Cyrus had used to make himself master of the place, and after a year and seven months, the army had become weary. Zopyrus, the son of the conspirator Megabyzus, was with the army, and, in the twentieth month of the siege, was astonished to find that one of his mules had, indeed, given birth to a foal. He remembered the taunts of the Babylonians and realised that some divine providence had fated that Babylon be taken. So he bade his servants keep their silence and went to Darius and asked if he valued highly the taking of Babylon. Darius confirmed that he did, indeed, desire to take Babylon, and Zopyrus reviewed all the ways to take the city and found one. He had himself maimed and mutilated in a way that was entirely without remedy by cutting off his own nose and ears and had himself flogged before bringing himself before the king.

Darius was outraged: 'What man has disfigured you thus so I might avenge you?' he asked of Zopyrus. 'There is no man but you, O King, who could reduce me to this plight: no stranger has done this. I have done it with my own hands, as I could no longer endure the fact that the Assyrians should laugh at the Persians', replied Zopyrus.

'Wretched man, you explain the foulest deed with good intentions, but a simpleton could see that you do not further our cause with this action', said Darius. Zopyrus now unveiled his plan: 'If I had told you my plan before executing it you would have stopped me, but please listen now, O Lord, and we shall take Babylon'.

Zopyrus planned to desert to the enemy and, taking advantage of his disfigurement and position in Persian society, convince the Babylonians to let him command a small number of troops. He urged Darius to wait until the tenth day and then attack the gates of Semiramis with a thousand poorly armed and expendable troops, then wait another seven days and attack the Nineveh gates with two thousand troops, and, after another twenty days, attack the Chaldaean gates with four thousand troops armed only with swords. Finally, Darius should then attack the city on all sides and bring two groups of Persians, one to the Belian gates and the other to the Cissian gates, where Zopyrus hoped to be in a position, because of his previous successes, to help the Persians through the gates and take the city.

Thus Zopyrus fled to the gates of Babylon, where the guards took him to the magistrates, who believed his story that Darius had punished him for his view that the siege should be raised because they had no hope of succeeding in taking the city. They were ready to give him the troops he asked for, as they were aware that he knew all the counsels of the Persian King and wanted revenge against him. Zopyrus prepared for the tenth day and sallied forth and slaughtered the thousand men that Darius had sent against the gate and accepted the praise of the Babylonians, who gave him command of more troops. Again, when the next period had elapsed, he slaughtered the two thousand men, and, after his victory over the four thousand, the Babylonians gave him command of their army and gave him the keys to the city.

Finally, Darius attacked as planned, and Zopyrus was able to throw open the gates, and the Persians took the city. Darius had three thousand of the leading citizens crucified and destroyed all of the gates. Fifty thousand women were brought in from the surrounding nations to replace the wives who had been strangled, and from these are the current inhabitants of Babylonia descended.

Darius honoured Zopyrus deeply and considered no Persian except Cyrus more worthy. 'Rather Zopyrus were unmaimed than twenty more Babylons', he would exclaim and he gave Zopyrus many gifts and the governorship of Babylon for life with no tribute, along with many other favours.

SCYTHIA

The Scythians had previously made themselves masters of Upper Asia for twenty-eight years after they defeated the Medes in battle. Those Scythians who had returned to their homes after almost thirty years found an army of slaves opposing them, for the womenfolk they had left behind had married their slaves. The Scythians are wont to blind their slaves and deploy them in large vats to help in the preparation of the mare's milk on which the Scythians largely subsist, by walking around until the milk separates, with the upper portion considered the best part. The Scythians also blind those whom they take in war, for they are a pastoral race and do not keep prisoners.

The sons of the slaves had grown and married the Scythian womenfolk and had no desire to be enslaved again. Because of this, they dug a broad trench from the Tauric mountains to Lake Maeotis and succeeded in defending themselves against the returning Scythians. The Scythians took counsel, and one of them addressed the rest: 'Why are we attacking our slaves, for many of us die in battle and we are killing people who belong to us. I suggest that we put aside our weapons and approach them with our horsewhips, for they consider themselves our equals when we are armed but will feel themselves our slaves if we approach them with just our whips'. So it was, and the slaves were so astounded by the approach of the unarmed Scythians that they forgot to fight and ran away, and the Scythians regained their lands after being lords of Asia for a time, but were then forced to abandon them by the Medes.

The Scythians claim that they are the youngest of all nations, founded in the desert one thousand years ago by Targitaus, the son of Jove, and a daughter of the

Borysthenes. Targitaus had three sons, and, during their reign, four golden objects fell from the sky: a plough, a yoke, a battle-axe and a drinking cup. As the eldest approached the objects, they burst into flames and could not be recovered. This was also the case for the second son. When the third son, Colaxais, approached, the flames were extinguished and the brothers agreed to hand the whole kingdom over to Colaxais. The sacred gold is guarded carefully, and a feast is held every year. The guardian of the gold must not fall asleep in the open air during this feast, or he is sure not to live out the year. His reward for guarding the gold is as much land as he can ride around on horseback in a day. Colaxais divided the kingdom into three for his three sons, although the kingdom containing the gold is larger than the other two.

The Greeks of the Pontus tell a different story and claim that the Scythians are descended from Hercules, who arrived in the region chased by a storm when he was carrying off the cows of Geryon and drew his lion's cloak around him and fell asleep. He had loosened his mares from his chariot to graze, and they wandered the length of the entire country. He searched for them, until he came across a strange lady in a cave who was half human and half serpent. He looked at her in wonder, and she admitted to having the mares and said that she would return them only if he made her his mistress. Hercules stayed with her only until she was ready to give the mares back, by which time she was pregnant. 'What shall I do with your sons', she asked, 'when they are born? Shall I keep them in this land or send them to you?' Hercules unslung a bow, for he carried two, and a belt and asked her to present them with a trial when they were old enough, and see who could draw the bow and thus become King of this land, and send the others away. In time, there were three sons, and their mother set forth the trial. Agathyrsus and Gelonus proved unequal to the task and were sent away, and the youngest, Scythes, drew the bow and became King and received the belt of Hercules, from which time it has been the custom of the Scyths to wear goblets attached to their belts.

I have heard a third explanation pertaining to the origin of the Scyths, and this I deem the most likely. The Scyths once dwelled in Asia but came to war with the Massagetae and crossed the river Araxes and then the land of the Cimmerians, half of whom fled, whereas the other half stayed to fight. The half who fought are now buried near the river Tyras, where the grave can still be seen. This explains why Scythia still has traces of the Cimmerians, and it seems that the Scyths pursued them but lost their trail and ended up confronting the Medes.

I can find no one who has visited the lands to the north to give me a description of the place, but Scythia is a land of several peoples, including the Callipedae and the Alazonians, who resemble the Scythians in their customs but also grow corn, garlic, lentils and millet. Next to the Alazonians are the cultivators who grow corn for trade, and then the Neuri, and beyond them the continent is uninhabited, as far as we know. There are other nations along the river Hypanis, including the woodland Hylaea and the Borysthenites, whose territory extends three days' journey to the river Panticapes, and northwards eleven days' journey by boat along the Borysthenes. Above this are the Cannibals, and then a vast uninhabited tract of desert. Crossing the Panticapes eastwards for fourteen days' journey to the river Gerrhus are the wandering Scythians, and across the Gerrhus lies the Royal district, containing the largest and bravest of the tribes, who regard all the other tribes as slaves. Their land reaches south to Taurica and east to the trench dug by the slaves to the river Tanais. North of the Royal Scythians are the Melanchaeni, who wear black robes and are of a different race, and that is the extent of our knowledge.

When you cross the Tanais, you are no longer in Scythia but in the land of the Sauromatae, which stretches for fifteen days' journey and is entirely bare of trees until you reach the land of the Budini, which is thickly wooded. North of here is seven days' journey across a desert, whereupon, somewhat to the east, you come across a populous nation called the Thyssagetae, and also the Iyrcae, who live by hunting, and, finally, to the east, a tribe of Scyths who once revolted from the Royal Scyths and migrated here.

This land is a smooth plain with deep soil, beyond which lies a rugged and stony region, in which the Argippaeans live at the foot of lofty mountains. They are said to be bald from birth, both men and women, and to have flat noses and long chins and to live off the fruit of the Ponticum, which is similar in size to our fig tree, with a fruit like a bean with a stone inside. They strain the juice of this fruit when it is ripe and mix it with milk and make it into solid cakes, which they eat instead of meat. All individuals belonging to this people live under their own tree, and nobody harms them, for people are considered sacred: when a quarrel occurs, it is quickly made up, and if anyone flees to them for refuge, he is safe from all hurt.

These lands which I have described have been explored in full by both the Greeks and Scythians. Those Scythians who make the journey from the Borysthenes communicate by means of seven languages and seven interpreters. Beyond the bald-headed people is said to be a race of men with feet like goats and, still further, a race of men who sleep during one half of the year. East of the bald-headed men are the Issedonians, who serve up the body of a father when he dies, mixed with the meat of a sheep, and all of the relatives eat it, whereas the head is cleansed and set in gold and brought out each year at a festival at which sons honour the lives of their fathers just as the Greeks celebrate Genesia. We hear from the Issedonians of one-eyed men and gold guarding griffins in the lands of their neighbours.

The entire district that I have described is subject to very cold winters lasting eight months out of the twelve, so cold that the sea freezes and the Cimmerian Bosphorus is frozen over. The Scythians who dwell inside the trench make war during the winter season and even drive their wagons over to the country of the Sindians. There is very little rain in the winter, and thunderstorms occur only in the summer. Horses can bear the cold, but mules cannot, and it seems to me that the cold prevents the oxen in Scythia from having horns. Hesiod and Homer mention a race called the Hyperboreans but I have not found a Scythian or a Greek who can confirm their existence. The people of Delos, however, claim that several virgins, along with gifts packed in straw, have come from the Hyperboreans into Scythia from which they have been passed on to Delos.

For my part, I laugh when I see people drawing maps of the world without any reason to guide them, making the ocean run right around the earth and the earth itself to be an exact circle as if drawn by a pair of compasses, with Europe and Asia the same size. The truth of the matter is that the Persians, Medes, Saspirians, and Colchians fill the whole space from the Erythraean Sea to the Northern Sea. West of this are two tracts of land, the first containing thirty different nations, beginning at the river Phasis in the north and stretching to the Myriandrian gulf adjoining Phoenicia in the south. The second tract to the west stretches from Persia, through Assyria, then Arabia, along the coast of Palestine-Syria until it comes to Egypt.

EXPEDITION TO SCYTHIA

Asia was rich in both men and gold, and so Darius decided to mount an expedition against the Scythians, who had previously made themselves masters of Upper Asia for twenty-eight years after they had defeated the Medes in battle. Darius began preparations for the expedition into Scythia, requesting some nations to furnish troops, and others to prepare ships, and making arrangements for a bridge to be built over the Thracian Bosphorus.

At this time, Oeobazus, a Persian and father of three sons all of whom were to accompany Darius to war, made a request that one of his sons should be excused military duty and allowed to remain at home. Darius answered as if he had made a friendly request and assured Oeobazus not to worry and that he would arrange for all his sons to remain with him, upon which Darius ordered his guards to take the three sons and put them to death before delivering them to his father in fulfilment of his promise.

Darius marched from Susa and surveyed the sea of Pontus, which is eleven thousand furlongs long and three thousand, three hundred wide but is just four furlongs wide at the mouth of a strait called the Bosphorus. This strait is one hundred and twenty furlongs in length, reaching from the Euxine to the Propontis, leading into the Hellespont and thence the Aegean. I have calculated these distances from the fact that a ship can travel about seventy thousand furlongs in a day. The Pontus also had a very large lake which is the mother of the sea called Lake Maeotis.

Darius now sailed to the Bosphorus, where a Samian, Mandrocles, had completed the bridge across the strait, and Darius was so pleased that he bestowed every gift tenfold onto the Samian with thanks and erected two marble pillars on which he inscribed the names of all of the nations that formed his army. Darius had drawn the army from all the nations under his sway. It was composed of seven hundred thousand men, including cavalry and six hundred ships. Mandrocles also commissioned a painting showing the bridge, and Darius seated, surveying the procession of his army, and dedicated it to the temple of Hera in Samos.

Darius now passed into Europe, having ordered the Ionians to sail to the mouth of the river Ister and build a bridge across the stream and await his coming. Darius marched on to the source of the river Tearus with his army and made camp there for three days. It is said that this river is charmed and that it will cure many diseases, and also cure any scab on man or beast, and Darius was so charmed by the river that he had another pillar erected. The army marched on and came to the river Artiscus, in the land of the Odrysians, where Darius ordered each man to throw a stone as he passed by, leaving behind great hills of stones created by the soldiers.

THRACE

The Thracians gave themselves up without a struggle, and as a result, the first people he subdued were the Getae, who obstinately defended themselves before they were enslaved. The Getae fire arrows into the sky when it thunders, uttering threats against the god, and they believe themselves immortal, for when they die they join their god, Zalmoxis.

Every five years they send messengers to their god by arranging darts on the ground and selecting one amongst them to be their messenger and throwing him up into the air so that he falls and impales himself on the darts. They impart their messages to the man as he is dying, and he takes them to their god and they think ill of the messenger if he does not die and pick another one to send away. I have been told by some Greeks that Zalmoxis was, in reality, a man, a slave from Samos, who had returned home and had built an underground chamber in his house to which he retired. After a period of three years, he re-emerged and caused much surprise amongst his countrymen, who now started to believe his philosophy that they would not die but go to a place filled with every conceivable form of good.

The Persian army came to the Ister and crossed on the bridge that the Ionians had made, whereupon Darius bade his naval troops break the bridge and follow him on land. The Mytilenaean General, Coes, counselled Darius to keep the bridge and have it guarded, for his fear was, not that they would be defeated by the Scythians, but that they might have trouble forcing them to engage in battle and that the bridge would be needed again for a return or for a retreat. So Darius tied sixty knots into a cord and handed it over to the Ionians, asking them to untie one knot a day while they were guarding the bridge and gave them leave to return to their homes when the last knot had been untied.

SCYTHIA

Scythia is square in shape, for it is ten days' journey from the Borysthenes to the Palus Maeotis, and a further ten days from the Palus Maeotis, and it is twenty days from the coast to the country of the Melanchaeni, who dwell above Scythia, where I estimate a day's journey to be two hundred furlongs. The Scythians realised that they were not strong enough to fight the Persians and consulted with their neighbours, the Tauri, the Agathyrsi, the Neuri, the Androphagi, the Melanchaeni, the Geloni, the Budini and the Sauromatae.

The Tauri live entirely on war and plundering and cut off the heads of their prisoners to stick on long poles outside their houses and throw the bodies off a cliff by their temple as an offering to their Goddess. The Agathyrsi are enamoured of luxury and wear a great deal of gold and hold all of their wives in common, so that they can all be brothers, the result being that one family cannot hate another. The Neuri are like other Scythians and were driven from their lands by a multitude of serpents. Both the Greeks and Scythians believe that each of the Neuri becomes a wolf for a few days each month before returning to their original form. The Androphagi are more savage than the others and have no laws and are the only people to practise cannibalism. The Melanchaeni wear black cloaks. The Budini are a large and powerful nation and have blue eyes and bright red hair. They possess a large city, called Gelonus, built of wood and surrounded by a wooden wall thirty furlongs on each side, probably built by Greeks who had fled to the Budini, for they worship Dionysus and their language is half-Greek, half-Scythian. The Geloni are tillers of the soil and have gardens and eat bread, whereas the Budini must be the original people of the land and are nomads.

It is reported that the Sauromatae are descended from Amazons who were taken prisoner by the Greeks at the battle of Thermodon and put on ships whose crews they overpowered and massacred, close to the shores of the Palus Maeotis. The Scythians fought an inconclusive battle with them and discovered that they were women. Because of this, they sent a detachment of their youngest men with orders to camp in the neighbourhood but to avoid fighting them, for they desired to obtain children from so noble a race. The Amazons were in the habit of scattering into groups of two or three at noon to go and relieve themselves, and the young men began to do the same.

After a few days, one of the young men approached one of the women and they became good friends, and she made him understand, though means of signs, to come again the next day with a friend. Soon all of the youths had gained the favour of the Amazons, and the two camps became one and the women learned the language of the men. The men wanted to return to their nation with their new wives, but the Amazons said: 'We could not live with your women, for our pursuits are different from theirs: we like to draw the bow, hurl the javelin and ride horses, and your women stay with your wagons and never hunt, and we should never get on. If you want to keep us as your wives, pray go to your parents and claim your inheritance and come back to us that we may live together'.

The youths thus claimed their inheritance and returned to the Amazons, who now asked them to move three days' journey over the Tanais mountains to where the Sauromatae now live. The women continue to observe their customs, accompanying their menfolk during hunting and in war, and they wear the same clothing as the men, and their law stipulates that a woman may not marry until she has killed a man in battle, so many women die unmarried having never fulfilled this condition.

JOURNEY AROUND SCYTHIA

The Kings of the neighbouring countries around Scythia assembled, and the envoy of the Scythians addressed them: 'Do not look on tamely on this conflict but join with us and meet the enemy, for the Persians come no less against you as against us. They have enslaved every nation they have passed through, intent on punishing us for invading Media. All of the tribes of the Thracians have been enslaved, and if the King had come against us only, he would not have molested any nation along the way'.

The Kings deliberated and were divided, with the Geloni, Budini and Sauromatae allying with the Scythians, and the Agathyrsi and Neurian princes and the kings of the Androphagi, Melanchaeni and Tauri withholding their support, on the grounds that the Scythians had been the aggressors against the Persians in the first place.

The Scythians now determined that they would not face the Persians in a pitched battle but would retire before them, driving off their herds and choking up the wells as they retreated, and leaving the earth bare of forage. They divided their forces into three bands, one of which was to retreat along the shores of the Palus Maeotis toward the Tanais mountains if the Persians advanced in that direction. The other two bands were to stay together and keep at a distance of a day's march from the Persians to prevent the latter from foraging successfully. They also planned to retreat toward those nations which had not agreed to form an alliance, in the hope of forcing them into the war.

The Scythians therefore sent their fleetest horsemen as scouts, who discovered the Persians three days' march from the Ister, and they destroyed all that grew on the ground and led the Persians toward the single division which was retreating toward the Tanais mountains, keeping their women and children in the wagons a day's march ahead of the Persians. They passed through the countries of the Scythians and the Sauromatae and came to the land of the Budini and the deserted city of Gelonus, which the Persians burned down. They passed through the land of the Budini to the desert, which has no inhabitants and extends for seven days' journey to the territory of the Thyssagetae, from whose lands great streams flow.

On reaching the desert, Darius halted and had eight large forts built sixty furlongs apart on the river Oarus and waited for the Scythian army to return. The Scythians had, however, followed another route and had re-entered Scythia and had, from the point of view of the Persians, disappeared.

Darius returned to Scythia and gave chase to the two combined divisions of the Scythians, who led him into the land of the Melanchaeni, who were greatly disturbed by the arrival, firstly, of the Scythian army, and, then, the Persian army. The latter was then led forth through the lands of the Androphagi and the Neuri, who were similarly distressed. The Scythians reached the land of the Agathyrsi, who sent heralds to the Scythians to forbid them from crossing their borders and massed their troops in preparation, whereupon the Scythians acquiesced and led the Persians back into Scythia.

Darius now sent a message to the Scythian King: 'O strange King, why do you continue to flee before my forces? If you think yourself stronger in battle, then let us engage in battle, and if you think your forces weaker, you have just to send me earth and water as your Lord for us to come to conference'. The Scythian replied: 'Persian, I fear no man nor flee from you, and there is nothing strange in what I do, as I am simply following our way of life. I am in no hurry to join in battle with you, as we have no towns or cultivated lands for you to ravage, but if you desire battle with us, you have but to find our fathers tombs and attempt to meddle with them and see whether or not we will fight. Until then we will not fight unless it pleases us to do so. As for my calling you Lord, I say "Go Weep".'

The Scythians now arranged a conference with the Ionians, who were guarding the bridge at the Ister, and stopped leading the Persians around the country, but harassed them while they were eating their meals or at night. They always managed to put the Persian cavalry to flight but were forced to retreat when faced with Persian foot soldiers. There was one thing which aided the Persians, and this was the braying of asses. This never failed to disconcert the Scythian horses, which were unaccustomed to the sound. The Scythians also let the Persians capture small numbers of cattle in an attempt to keep them in Scythia while they negotiated with the Ionians with regard to the bridge.

Darius was now at his wits' end, and the Scythian King sent him a message, along with presents, which were a bird, a mouse, a frog and five arrows, but offered no explanation as to their meaning. Darius thought that this meant that the Scythians were going to surrender because the mouse signified the earth, the frog water, and the arrows the surrender of all of their power. Gobryas, one of the seven conspirators, however, saw the message in another light: 'Unless you Persians can burrow into the earth or fly into the sky or hide in the water, we will destroy you with our arrows'.

Meanwhile, a single band of Scythians had approached the Ionians and offered freedom to Ionia if they departed from the bridge and went home after sixty days had passed and they had fulfilled the promise to Darius. They received the agreement of the Ionians and hastened back with all speed. The remaining Scythian army now drew itself out into formation, facing the Persians and ready for battle.

Now it happened that a hare sprang up and was running between the lines, whereupon the Scythians who saw it rushed off in pursuit. Darius wondered what the noise was about and was told that half of the Scythian cavalry had rushed off to chase a hare. He turned to his nobles saying: 'These men despise us utterly, and I think that Gobryas was right about the meaning of the gifts. I see now that it is time to secure safe passage back to our homes'. Gobryas advised: 'I am convinced that the Scythians are making game of us and that we must retreat before our foes march toward the Ister and destroy the bridge. I counsel that we light our fires as usual tonight but begin the retreat under cover of darkness'.

HISTIAEUS

Darius took all of his fighting troops, leaving behind the sick men and the asses, the latter continuing to bray all night, and telling the soldiers who were left behind that they were off to attack the Scythians. The next morning these men realised that they had been betrayed, and the Scythians and their allies saw that the Persians had gone, and set off at once in pursuit and headed straight for the Ister. Now it happened that the Scythians travelled much faster than the Persians, and by a more direct route, and came to the bridge before the Persians and urged the Ionians to go home.

Miltiades, the Athenian, recommended that the Ionians do as the Scythians had asked and bring themselves freedom, but Histiaeus, the Milesian, objected on the grounds that, once free, the Ionians were sure to prefer democracy over kingly rule and the kings and princes present would all lose their privileges and become common citizens. All of the captains there were high in the esteem of the Persian King and were the tyrants and princes of the Ionian cities, and all voted with Histiaeus.

The Ionians, however, began to dismantle the bridge on the Scythian side, appearing thus to support the Scythians, and bade them seek out the Persian army. The Scythians had scourged the land as they went and believed that the Persians would follow a route which offered forage and water and missed the Persian army for a second time as a consequence. The Persians had simply kept to their route and not departed from it, whereupon they reached the bridge and, seeing it dismantled, thought, in terror, that the Ionians had abandoned them.

Darius bade an Egyptian, who had a very loud voice, hail Histiaeus, who immediately brought the fleet to assist and made good the bridge, allowing the Persian army across before the Scythian army could confront them. Because of this, the Scythians still taunt the Ionians as being the most dastardly of men as free men but the most loyal people as slaves.

Darius and his army passed back through Thrace, and on into Asia, leaving Megabazus on the European side in charge of an army of eighty thousand men, where he proceeded to subdue all of the nations which had not already been brought under control by the Medes.

EXPEDITION TO ATHENS

Darius used the war between the Eginetans and the Athenians as a pretext for carrying the fight into Greece and reducing all of those nations who had not offered him earth and water. He appointed new generals: a Mede called Datis, and his nephew, Artaphernes, with orders to capture Athens and her ally, Eretria, and bring the people captive into his presence.

The commanders set sail from Cilicia with six hundred triremes containing a large land army and horse transports, and journeyed via Samos to the island of Naxos, which the Persians had previously failed to subdue. The Naxians abandoned their towns in fear, and the Persians took prisoners and burned all of their temples, along with the town, before sailing on to other islands.

Datis discovered that the people of Delos had fled their island, whereupon he sent them a message: 'Holy Men, how wrongly you have judged me, for surely you know I would spare the island that has given birth to two gods?' So the Delians returned, but their island was shaken by an earthquake, as God had warned them of the calamities that would befall the Greeks at the hands of the Persians over the next twenty years.

ERETRIA

The Persians sailed against Eretria, with their army supplemented by the Ionians and Aeolians, and troops taken at each island they conquered on the way. The Persians were refused only by the island of Carystus, which was put under siege and wasted until the inhabitants relented and agreed to do what was desired of them.

The Eretrians waited for the Persians and sought assistance from the Athenians, who sent them four thousand landowners to whom they had allotted estates in Euboea. The Eretrians did not agree among themselves whether they should fight the Persians or flee to the mountains, and some even plotted to betray their country. Aeschines, one of the first men in Eretria, bade the Athenians flee over the water to Oropus. The Persian navy then arrived and anchored nearby at Tamynae, Choereae and Aegilia. The Persians set forth and laid siege to the fortress of Eretria, which was assaulted over six days until the city was betrayed and plundered and the temples burnt and the people made captive, in accordance with the orders of Darius.

BATTLE OF MARATHON

The Persians now went forth to capture the city of Athens and set sail for Marathon, which was a suitable place for their cavalry to attack the Athenians. The Athenian army, led by Miltiades, received intelligence of the Persian plan and awaited their arrival.

Now Cimon, the father of Miltiades, had been banished from Athens by Pisistratus and subsequently managed to win the four-horse chariot race at the Olympiad three times. On the second occasion, he caused Pisistratus to be named winner in return for being allowed to return to Athens. He was killed by the sons of Pisistratus after the third occasion on which he won. It was this Miltiades, the son of Cimon, who had been elected the Athenian general by the people.

The Athenians had dispatched a messenger called Pheidippides to Sparta, who arrived on the very next day after he had departed Athens and was visited by the god Pan on his journey, causing the Athenians to build a temple to him under the Acropolis and to hold yearly sacrifices and a torch race in his honour. Pheidippides was brought before the rulers of Sparta and gave the following message: 'Men of Lacedaemon, the Athenians beseech you to hasten to their aid and not allow this most ancient state in the whole of Greece to be enslaved by the Persians, who have already carried away the people of Eretria captive'. Now the Spartans wished to help Athens, but their customs forbade them from marching out of Sparta until the next full moon.

The Persians were conducted to Marathon by Hippias, the son of Pisistratus, who had seen a vision in which he was restored to Athens and his power recovered. As he landed at Marathon, he sneezed and, as he was an old man, several of his teeth fell out into the sand and could not be recovered. He realised that his dream was void and that the only part of the land that would be his was the portion of which his teeth had possession.

The Athenians were drawn up for battle in a sacred close dedicated to Heracles and were joined by their allies, the Plataeans. The Athenian generals were in disagreement, as a number of them thought that they were too few to face a host as great as the Medes. Miltiades saw that the vote might go against combat and sought out the Polemarch of Athens, who held the casting vote. 'Callimachus, it lies with you to decide between freedom and slavery, for never have the Athenians been in such danger as now. If we bow to the yoke of the Medes, we will suffer under the power of Hippias, but if we fight and win, Athens will be raised to be the first city in Greece. The generals are divided in their vote, and you have to cast the vote either for conflict, which might make us free, and the first city in Greece, or the reverse'. So

Miltiades won him over, and Callimachus cast his vote in favour of battle.

The Athenians were drawn up, with Callimachus in command of the right wing: then came an unbroken line of the Athenian tribes, with the Plataeans forming the left wing. To make their line equal in length to that of the Persians, they weakened the centre and strengthened the wings to a depth of many ranks. With both armies facing each other at a distance of eight furlongs and ready for battle, the Athenians charged the barbarians at a run. These were the first Greeks to charge the enemy at a run and the first Greeks to face men clad in Medean battle armour, and the Persians must have thought them mad to attack without horsemen or archers.

The two armies fought on the plain of Marathon for a length of time, and the Persians broke through the centre of the Greek line and pursued the Greeks, but on the wings the Plataeans and the Athenians, having defeated the enemy, fell upon those who had broken the centre, and fought and conquered them. The Persians fled and were chased by the Athenians, who cut them down and chased them all the way to the ships and called for fire. Callimachus was killed, as was Stesilaus, the son of one of the generals, and the son of Euphorion, who perished after having his hand cut off, together with many other Athenians of note and name.

The Athenians succeeded in securing seven ships, but the remainder set sail and took aboard their Eretrian prisoners before sailing around Cape Sounion, hoping to reach the city of Athens before the Athenian army could return. The Athenian army marched at all possible speed back to Athens and returned before the Persian fleet reached Phalerum, which was the port of Athens. After resting on their oars and seeing that the Athenian army faced them, the Persians sailed away for Asia.

About six thousand, four hundred men fell on the side of the barbarians at the battle of Marathon, and one hundred and ninety-two on the side of the Athenians. A strange tale was recounted by an Athenian, Epizelus, who found himself blinded during the battle: a gigantic warrior with a huge beard, which cast a shadow over his entire shield, stood over him and slew the men at his side.

Datis and Artaphernes returned to Asia and took the Eretrians whom they held captive to Darius, at Susa, who treated them well and had them settled in Cissia, two hundred and ten furlongs from Susa, at a place at which they could extract bitumen, salt and oil from the earth, where the oil is black and has an unpleasant smell, referred to as 'rhadinacé' by the Persians.

The Lacedaemonians came to Athens after the full moon and took just three days to arrive from Sparta but they came too late for the battle and continued their march to Marathon in order to view the slain Medean army. They gave the Athenians fulsome praise for their achievement and then returned home.

PAROS

The Athenians held Miltiades in such high esteem after the battle of Marathon that he was able to ask for a fleet of seventy ships with armed men and money without even telling them whom he was going to attack. He merely promised to enrich those who accompanied him and, as soon as he had obtained the armament he had requested, he set sail with his force for the island of Paros, against which he had a grudge. His excuse for attacking the Parians was that they had supplied a trireme to accompany the Persian fleet at Marathon, but the truth was that a Parian called Tisias had told tales against him to Hydarnes the Persian.

Miltiades arrived with his force at Paros and laid siege to the people, who had locked themselves up inside the town. Miltiades demanded payment of a hundred talents to leave them be, but the Parians refused and defended their citadel in a variety of ways, including rebuilding their walls every night in the places at which they thought they might be attacked.

The Parians claim that Miltiades was at his wits' end, when Timo, one of their priestesses, offered to show him a means of taking the city and led him into the temple of Demeter, which was located on a hill in front of the city. He was unable to open the door but leapt over a fence into the temple precinct, perhaps intending to remove some holy things, although it was not permitted for a man to enter the temple. Miltiades was filled with dread as he reached the door to the temple and returned the way he had come, but they say that he struck his knee while jumping down from the outer wall as he was leaving.

Miltiades was forced to return to Athens with no money, sick from the wound in his knee, having besieged the Parians for twenty-six days but gaining no reward. The Parians sent to Delphi to ask the Oracle how to punish their priestess for trying to betray them to the Athenians and showing to Miltiades mysteries which it was not lawful for a man to know. The Oracle forbade them to punish Timo, for she had lured Miltiades to his destruction.

Miltiades was brought to trial in Athens and was unable to defend himself because of his wound. His friends represented him and made much of his record in the fight at Marathon, and also, previously, when he had led the forces which took Lemnos. Miltiades was found guilty, however, and died soon afterwards, when his wound became gangrenous, leaving his son, Cimon, to pay the fine of fifty talents.

LEMNOS

Let me finish with the tale of how Miltiades had made himself master of Lemnos.

The Athenians had given a people called the Pelasgi some worthless land near Athens in payment for a wall which the Pelasgians had built.

The Pelasgians cultivated and improved the land until the Athenians begrudged them this and drove them out, with the excuse that they were abusing Athenian children as they collected water from a nearby fountain.

The Athenians, according to the historian Hecataeus, claimed that the Pelasgians plotted against them but spared their lives and forced them to abandon Attica, and they eventually settled on the island of Lemnos. The Pelasgians now avenged themselves by carrying off many Athenian women during a festival and making them their wives. These wives taught their children the Athenian customs and language, and it transpired that all of the youths would protect one other if one of their number was threatened by one of the Pelasgian children.

The Pelasgians saw this and became concerned about what might happen when these children grew to adulthood and had the children and their mothers slain. After this, their lands failed to bear fruit and their wives had fewer children and their herds increased more slowly than before, until they had to send men to Delphi and received the message that they must ask Athens for whatever satisfaction they might demand for the crimes they had committed.

The Athenians prepared a table laden with fruits and demanded that the Pelasgians deliver their lands up to the Athenians in a similar state, which the Pelasgians refused to do 'until a ship came from Athens to their country on a north wind within a single day', which they knew was impossible.

Many years later, during the prevalence of the Etesian winds, Miltiades sailed his ship to Lemnos within a day and called on the Pelasgians to leave the island in accordance with the prophecy. Some of the people obeyed, and some were besieged and brought over by force, and thus Miltiades and the Athenians gained Lemnos.

XERXES

The anger of King Darius against the Athenians grew and grew in the wake of the Athenian attack on Sardis, and once he heard of the defeat of the Persian forces at Marathon, he started preparations to lead an army himself into Greece and enslave the Athenians. All of Asia was in commotion, as levies were increased and ships, horses, transports and provisions prepared. In the fourth year the Egyptians revolted and Darius desired to march an army against both adversaries.

Persian law demanded that the Persian King leave behind an heir before he went to war, and Darius had three sons from his first wife, who was a daughter of Gobryas, and four sons from Atossa the daughter of Cyrus. Artabazanes was the eldest son of the former, and Xerxes the eldest son of the latter, and these two were now in contention to become the legitimate heir.

It happened that Demaratus, the son of a deposed and banished Spartan king, came to Susa and advised Xerxes that the law in Sparta would favour Xerxes' claim, for Artabazanes was born before Darius became King, and only Xerxes was, therefore, of royal blood. Xerxes succeeded in persuading Darius that he had justice on his side, but I believe that the power of Atossa, who was the daughter of Cyrus and who had also been the wife of Cambyses, probably influenced this outcome, and Xerxes became the heir to the kingdom.

Darius died in the year following the Egyptian revolt before he could complete the preparation of his armies, and Xerxes now became King of the Persians. Xerxes was cold to the idea of bringing war to the Greeks but his cousin, Mardonius, the son of Gobryas, urged him to lead an army against Athens once he had subdued Egypt.

Mardonius sought adventure and hoped that the satrapy of Greece would fall to him.

Xerxes marched first against the Egyptians, in the year following the death of Darius, and subdued them, and made his brother, Achaemenes, governor, and the latter ruled more severely than his father.

Xerxes now called the Persian nobles together and explained his desire to rival the exploits of Cyrus, Cambyses and Darius by building a bridge over the Hellespont and marching an army through Europe against Greece. Not only had the Athenians offended Persia by attacking Sardis and defeating Datis and Artaphernes at Marathon, but, once all of the nations of Europe had been subdued, there would be no nation in the world capable of taking up arms against Persia. Xerxes then appealed to the nobles to speak freely about his plans.

Mardonius spoke first, declaring the view that the Persians had nothing to fear from the Greeks, for he himself had passed through Macedonia and almost reached Athens without having to face the Greeks in battle. The Persians need not fear the numbers nor the wealth of the Greeks, and, in any case, the Greeks themselves, although speaking a common language, were unable to communicate and make up their differences, and were constantly seeking out a plain on which to assemble and fight, often with great losses on both sides. Mardonius thought that the Greeks might not even dare to meet the Persians in battle, but that, if they did, a carefully prepared army could overcome them.

None of the other nobles ventured to offer an opinion, and Artabanus, the son of Hystaspes, given that he was the uncle of Xerxes, therefore proffered the opposite opinion, reminding Xerxes that he had advised Darius not to attack the Scyths and to remember how the

Persian army might have suffered disaster if Histiaeus had not stayed loyal and protected the bridge over the Ister. He pointed out that the Greek navy might sail to the proposed bridge at the Hellespont and destroy it, and cause problems for the Persian army in Europe. He counselled Xerxes to break up the meeting so he could give the matter serious thought, before coming to a conclusion – and that, in any case, he should not lead the army in person.

Xerxes thought on the matter and at first began to think that it was not to his advantage to lead the army into Greece, but he had a vision in the night in which a tall and beautiful man admonished him for changing his mind. Nevertheless, he announced to the nobles that he had decided not to make war on the Greeks after all, but then had a second vision, in which he was admonished again for changing his mind and not bringing war to Greece.

Xerxes grew frightened and sent for Artabanus and had him wear his clothes and sit on the throne and sleep in his bed to see if the same vision would visit him in his sleep. Artabanus had a similar vision, in which he was threatened for dissuading Xerxes from attacking the Greeks, and, as the man in his vision tried to burn out his eyes, he awoke and ran shrieking to Xerxes and gave him a full account of the vision. So Xerxes called the nobles together again and Artabanus changed his mind, and now all favoured the expedition against Athens.

Preparations began, and it was not until the fifth year after the recovery of Egypt that Xerxes set forward to march his army to Greece. Previous expeditions were nothing in comparison with this, for Xerxes called upon all the nations of Asia to furnish him with men, or ships, or cavalry, or provisions. The Persian fleet had previously met with disaster at Athos, and Xerxes had a trench dug across the land for the ships to sail down rather than have them carried. Perhaps it was vanity on his part to create a canal when the ships could have been carried, but this shows the greatness of his power. A bridge was built over the river Strymon, and provisions laid down in many places along the path that the army was to take into Greece.

The army gathered in Critalla in Cappadocia and marched with Xerxes toward Sardis, crossing the river Halys, where they reached the city of Celaenae. Here, a man called Pythius entertained Xerxes and his entire army and offered to give a sum of money toward the war. Xerxes enquired about the man, for no one else had offered him such gifts, and he was given to understand that Pythius was the wealthiest man in the world, save the King. Xerxes questioned Pythius and ascertained that his wealth was two thousand silver talents and seven thousand short of four million gold coins. Xerxes was impressed and swore friendship with Pythius and offered to lend him the seven thousand coins so that Pythius could donate a round four million to the war.

THE PERSIAN ARMY MARCHES

The army proceeded through to the city of Colossae in Phrygia, and on to Cydrara, on the Lydian border, across the river Maeander to Callatebus, and then on to the Lydian capital of Sardis. Xerxes now sent messengers everywhere to demand earth and water from those states that had previously refused, although he sent no messengers to Athens or Sparta. Xerxes heard that a great storm had destroyed the bridge he had had built over the Hellespont, and he was so enraged that he ordered that the waters should receive a hundred lashes and that a pair of fetters should be cast into the water. Some say he ordered the water branded with red hot irons. The engineers paid for this misfortune with their heads.

A pair of bridges was now constructed, with 360 boats floated out on one side and 315 on the other, and lashed together and held with great anchors. A gap was left between each penteconter so that light craft could navigate through, and six cables ran along each bridge, two of flax and four of papyrus, tightened with the help of wooden capstans. Planks were laid on the bridge, and then brushwood and earth trodden down, and a wooden wall built on either side of the causeway to prevent the animals from seeing the water and taking fright.

The army wintered at Sardis, and the bridges and the canal at Athos were made ready. The army set forth for Abydos in the spring. As they departed, the sun suddenly disappeared and day turned into night, and Xerxes sent for the Magi, who interpreted this as a portent of the destruction of the Greeks. As the army set forth, Pythius, who was made bold by the many gifts he had given Xerxes, asked if the eldest of his five sons could remain with him in Lydia while the other four went with the army. Xerxes was enraged at his presumption, particularly as Xerxes himself and his kinsfolk were going with the army. He granted his wish and had the eldest son found and cut in half, with each half placed on either side of the road so that the army could march through the two halves.

The baggage bearers and the beasts of burden went first, and then a vast crowd of many nations comprising about half the army. An empty space followed between them and the King, and then came a thousand horsemen, followed by a thousand spearmen walking with their spears pointing to the ground. Then came the ten sacred Nisaean horses which always accompanied the Persian army. Next came the chariot of Zeus, drawn by eight milk-white steeds, and then Xerxes in a chariot with his charioteer, Patiramphes, the son of Otanes. Then one thousand spearmen with their lances held in the usual manner, pointing upwards, and a thousand cavalry, followed by the ten thousand picked foot soldiers. Now came another ten thousand Persian cavalry, and, after a distance of two furlongs, the rest of the army followed in a confused crowd.

XERXES WEEPS

The army left Lydia and travelled on through the land of Mysia to the base of Mount Ida, where a storm killed no small number of men. They reached the river Scamander, which failed them and could not satisfy the thirst of the men and beasts. Here Xerxes ascended the Pergamus of Priam and offered a thousand oxen to the Trojan Athena in memory of the heroes slain at Troy. The army now reached Abydos, and Xerxes had a throne built upon a hill, so that he could behold in one view his whole army and navy arraigned before him. He arranged a sailing match, and, as he viewed the Hellespont, covered with his fleet and with his army on the plain below, he marvelled at his good fortune but soon began to weep.

Artabanus enquired of the great King why he wept, and Xerxes replied: 'there came upon me a sudden pity when I thought of the shortness of a man's life, for not one of the men I see will be alive when one hundred years has gone by'. Artabanus observed: 'and yet there are sadder things than that, for every man has thought more than once in his life that he wished himself dead, for there are many things that vex and harass us and make life, short though it be, appear long'. 'True enough, Artabanus, human life is as you say, but let us turn away from these thoughts and tell me, as you view the army and navy before us, would you still try to dissuade me from this expedition against Greece?' asked Xerxes. 'I see two dangers', replied Artabanus, 'the land and the sea. For there is no harbour big enough for all of your ships, and, as the army travels further, the land will become a danger, as it may produce a famine'. This prompted the reply from Xerxes: 'There is reason in your counsel, but success attends the boldest for the most part and not those who weigh everything and are slow to act. We set forward at the best season of the year with vast stores of provisions and we shall have the grain of the nations we conquer'. He then sent Artabanus back to Susa and gathered the Persian nobles together to pray to the gods for their success.

The army now began to cross the Hellespont over the two bridges, and the crossing took seven days, while the fleet sailed westwards to await the army at Cape Sarpedon. The army followed the path of the river Chersonese, passing through a town called Agora, over the river Melas, and then westwards, past Lake Stentoris, and on to the plain at Doriscus, where there was a Persian fort garrisoned from the time of the Scythian expedition. Here the sea captains beached and repaired their ships, and Xerxes began a review and a counting of the troops.

COMPOSITION OF THE ARMY

These were the nations that took part in the expedition.

The Persians wore soft hats and trousers and tunics with sleeves of different colours, covered with iron scales, like those of a fish, using wicker shields with a quiver hanging from their backs and a large bow with reed arrows and a short spear and a dagger hanging from a belt on their right thighs. The Medes and the Hyrcanians had the same dress, as did the Cissians, although the latter wore turbans on their heads. The Assyrians wore linen corselets, with brass helmets plaited in a strange fashion, and carried shields, lances, and daggers and wooden clubs studded with iron. The Bactrians had headgear similar to that of the Medes but were armed with bows made of cane and short spears. The Scythians wore trousers and tall, stiff pointed hats, with their bows, and a dagger and a battle axe. The Indians wore cotton dresses, with their bows and arrows tipped with iron. The Arians carried Median bows but were otherwise equipped like the Bactrians. The Parthians, Chorasmians, Sogdians, Gandarians, and Dadicae were also dressed like the Bactrians. The Caspians had cloaks made of animal skins and carried their own style of bow and a scimitar. The Sarangians had bright garments and buskins which reached to the knee, with Median bows and lances. The Pactyans, Utians, Mycians, and Paricanians wore skins and a particular style of bow and a dagger. The Arabians wore a long cloak fastened with a belt and carried long bows which bent backwards when unstrung. The Ethiopians wore leopard or lion skins and long bows no less than four cubits in length, with short arrows made of reeds and tipped with a sharp stone, and spears with sharpened animal horns for points and clubs, and they painted their bodies half white and half vermillion when they went into battle. The Libyans wore leather, with javelins that had been hardened in fire. The Paphlagonians wore plaited helmets and small shields and spears, as did the Ligyans and the Syrians, and the Phrygians and the Armenians. The Lydians and Mysians were dressed like Greeks, and the Thracians wore fox skins on their heads and tunics, with a long cloak of many colours with javelins and short daggers. Soldiers from the

Chalybians, Cabalians, Milyans, Moschians, Mares and Colchians also formed part of the army.

Six generals commanded the whole of the infantry, with the exception of the ten thousand who were known as 'the immortals', for when one of them fell, his place was immediately filled by another man, and their number was always, therefore, exactly ten thousand. The Persian troops were magnificently adorned with a large amount of gold and were also the bravest, and were followed by litters containing their concubines and their attendants and camels carrying their provisions. All of these nations fight on horseback, but only the Persians, Sagartians, Medes and Cissians, Indians, Bactrians and Caspians, Libyans, Caspeirians and Paricanians and the Arabians supplied cavalry to the army, who were commanded by two sons of Datis.

The fleet consisted of twelve hundred and seven triremes supplied by the Phoenicians and Syrians, the Egyptians, Cyprians, and Cilicians, and smaller numbers from the Pamphylians, Lydians, Dorians of Asia, Carians, and Ionians, and each had a band of soldiers on board.

Xerxes reviewed the troops and then sent for Demaratus, who had previously marched into Greece, and asked him if he thought that the Greeks would fight when faced with such a mighty force. 'O King! Would you like a true answer or a pleasant one?' he asked, and prompted for the truth, he answered: 'Brave are all the Greeks, but the Lacedaemonians of Sparta, in particular, will never accept any terms which would reduce them to slavery, and even if only one thousand of them took to the field they would surely meet you in battle'. 'We also have men of valour', said Xerxes: 'for each of the ten thousand would fight against three Greeks', and the army marched on into Thrace.

THESSALY

The whole area as far as the borders of Thessaly had already been subdued by the conquests of Megabazus and Mardonius. Xerxes crossed the dry channel to the Lissus and passed the cities of Maroneia, Dicaea, and Abdera and Lake Ismaris and Lake Stryme and the city of Pistyrus. All of these cities were coastal, and Xerxes kept them on the left-hand side as he passed by with the army. He reached the river Strymon, near the city of Eion, where Boges was governor, and the Magi sacrificed white horses to make the stream favourable. The army crossed the river and proceeded westwards to the town of Argilus and across the Sylean plain to Acanthus, where many Greeks were made to join the army and given gifts of Median dress. Artachaeus, who was one of the tallest of the Persians, and well known to Xerxes, died here, causing Xerxes to grieve.

Xerxes had to be entertained, and the army fed wherever they went, and Antipater of Thasos estimated the cost at four hundred talents of silver for one meal. Corn and wheat and barley was stored up for many months, and cattle and fish and poultry prepared, together with gold and silver drinking cups and other eating utensils for the royal table. A tent was also prepared for the royal party, and after the army and the royal guests had spent the night, everything was taken away when the army departed. Megacreon of Abdera wittily urged his people to give thanks to the gods for sparing them one half of their woes, for Xerxes and the army had stopped for just one meal and departed before breakfast, saving the town from ruin.

The fleet now separated from the land force and passed through the channel that had been dug at Athos and rounded Cape Ampelus and received a number of ships and men from each of the cities that it passed, including Torone, Galepsus, Sermyla, Mecyberna and Olynthus. From here they voyaged on to their destination and anchored off the Axius and off Therma, and at the towns in between, having received more ships and men as they passed the cities of Potidaea, Aphytis, Neapolis, Aega, Therambus, Scione, Mende and Sane, and also Lipaxus, Combreia, Lisae, Gigonus, Campsa, Smila and Aenea.

Xerxes marched the army in three bodies to the town of Therma, meeting no resistance apart from the region near the river Echeidorus, which is full of lions and wild bulls, where the lions chose to attack only the camels. The army now camped along the coast, stretched out from the city of Therma as far as the rivers Lydias and Haliacmon, and Xerxes surveyed the Thessalian mountains Olympus and Ossa.

Xerxes now took a boat to the mouth of the river Peneus and discovered that the whole of Thessaly was surrounded by mountains and that five rivers poured into a gorge which looked as if it had been created by an earthquake sent by Poseidon. He observed that it was no wonder that the Thessalians had brought him earth and water, for one had only to seal up the river with an embankment to flood the whole of Thessaly. Earth and water had, by now, arrived from all of the communities in Thessaly with the exception of Plataea and Thespiae.

Xerxes sent no messengers to Athens because the previous messengers who had been sent by Darius had been thrown into a deep pit and told to get the earth and water and take it themselves to their King if they could.

The Spartans also threw the messengers into a well, but, from that moment onward, their sacrifices failed to prompt any good signs and two volunteers offered themselves to be sent to the Persian King as atonement for the slaying of the messengers. Sperthias and Bulis gave themselves up and were brought into the presence of Xerxes at Susa, where they refused to bow or prostrate themselves, for they were free men. Xerxes however did not want to wipe the stain of the killing of the Persian messengers by doing the same to the Spartans and he let them go free.

THE GREEKS PREPARE FOR WAR

I think that if the Athenians had not decided to resist the Persians and had either quit their land or offered earth and water to Xerxes, then there would have been no ships to face the Persian navy and the land army would have conquered the whole of Greece. There would have been a barricade across the isthmus leading to the Peloponnese, but the Spartans would have stood alone and fought and died bravely, or come to terms with the Persians. Either way, the whole of Greece would have been subdued.

The Athenians knew that the Persian army was coming and had consulted the Oracle and had been advised by the Pythoness to 'flee and abandon your homes, for all is ruined and lost, and many towers will be levelled and the shrines of the gods will be destroyed by fire, for impetuous Ares hastens to destroy Athens, and black blood is already dripping from the high rooves as a sign of your imminent destruction'.

The Athenians went back with olive branches and begged the Oracle for something more comforting, and the Pythoness replied that 'Pallas Athena has not been able to soften the will of the lord of Olympus but Zeus grants that, once the foe have taken what they want from Athens, do not expect safety from men or horse, but you and your children will be kept safe by a wooden wall. So turn your back and retreat from the foe, for one day you will meet them in battle'.

A debate raged on the precise meaning of these messages, until the view of Themistocles, who argued that the 'wooden wall' represented the navy and that the Athenians should board their ships and fight the Persians at sea, prevailed. Themistocles had previously persuaded the Athenians to use a large sum of money obtained from their silver mines at Laureium to build two hundred ships to use in their war against the Eginetans, and these ships would now help Athens in her hour of need. Orders were given to build more ships, and the Athenians decided to take their entire force to sea.

The Greeks decided to end any feuds among themselves, and so the war between the Athenians and the Eginetans came to a close. As Xerxes brought his army to Sardis, ambassadors were sent to Argos, Sicily, Corcyra and Crete in an attempt to unite the Greek forces as one. Spies were sent to Asia and were caught and about to be executed when Xerxes thought it better that they be shown the extent of the Persian forces and be allowed to report back to the Greeks and apprise them of the vastness of his army. He followed similar logic when he saw some merchant ships at Abydos taking corn to the Peloponnese and he wondered: 'What harm are they doing, for they are carrying our provisions there for us?'.

The Athenian ambassadors first went to Argos, where the people were suffering, having lost six thousand citizens not long before, in a conflict with the Lacedaemonians under Cleomenes. The Argives had already sent to Delphi, and the reply was that they would help 'if the Lacedaemonians firstly made a truce for thirty years and divided the leadership of the army, although strictly the Argives should be in charge of the army', for they greatly desired a truce which would give their sons time to come to manhood. The Spartans replied that 'Sparta has two kings, and Argos but one, so it was possible for the Argive King to have one vote like each of them without their Kings losing any dignity'. The Greeks say that the Persians had sent heralds to Argos claiming friendship because the Persians were descended from Perseus and Danae, who had been the Lords of Argos, and the Argives had, therefore, given their reply while knowing that the Spartans could not agree on the issue of leadership.

GELO

Gelo of Syracuse in Sicily had made his city great by razing the cities of Camarina and Megara and bringing the rich people to Syracuse, where he established them as citizens, and selling the common people as slaves to be sent abroad. He did the same with the Euboeans of Sicily, and, in this way, became a great King.

Gelo had a large army under his command, and the Athenian and Lacedaemonian ambassadors begged him to come to the aid of Greece, but Gelo remembered a slight when he had asked to be avenged on the people of Egesta for their murder of Dorieus during his conflict with Carthage and had received no help.

However, he made them an offer: 'I am ready to give you aid and I have two hundred triremes, twenty thousand men at arms, two thousand cavalry and the same number of archers, with enough corn for your whole army, although I ask just one condition - that I be appointed chief captain and commander of the Greek forces during this war with the barbarian'.

The Spartans remonstrated at this request, and Gelo reconsidered and offered to accept leadership of either the army or the navy, at which point the Athenian envoy countered that 'even if the Spartans were willing to offer Gelo the leadership of the navy, the Athenians would not agree, for why should command be taken away from the most ancient nation in Greece and the only Greeks who had never changed their abode?'

Gelo addressed the ambassadors: 'You seem to have no shortage of commanders, but you are likely to lack the men to take their orders for, as you claim everything and offer nothing, I am unable to help you and suggest that you return to Greece and tell her that her finest troops are denied her'.

As soon as the Persians had crossed the Hellespont, Gelo sent three penteconters with a large amount of money to Delphi, with orders given to their captain, Cadmus, to observe the war and give the treasure and earth and water to Xerxes if he won, but to return with the treasure if the Greeks won the day. Cadmus was an honourable man who had handed over his kingly power at Cos to the people and had proven honest enough to be in charge of such a treasure. Those who live in Sicily say that Gelo would have come to the aid of the Greeks if he had not had to fight a large army brought to Sicily under the command of Hamilcar, the King of the Carthaginians.

The Corcyraeans promised to come to the aid of the Greeks, 'not wishing to stand by and see Greece fall, for the next day they would have to submit to slavery', and they sent sixty ships, but the ships went no further than the Peloponnese and stayed anchored near Pylos and took no part in the war.

The Cretans sent to Delphi and subsequently also decided not to join with the Greeks, and so the alliances were concluded.

FIRST CONTACT

The Thessalians did not join the cause of the Medes until they were forced to do so by the arrival of the Persian army, and sent envoys offering to send a strong force to guard the pass of Olympus as part of a combined resistance with the Greeks. The Greeks collected a force of ten thousand men and sailed up to Alus and marched into Thessaly, commanded by Evaenetus of Sparta and Themistocles of Athens, where they were joined by Thessalian cavalry.

After a few days, however, they received intelligence on the size of the Persian army and decided to retreat and defend the isthmus of the Peloponnese instead. My opinion is that they feared that the Persians might come through another pass by the town of Gonnus, and, soon afterwards, this was the path which Xerxes took into Thessaly.

The Greeks now decided to defend the pass at Thermopylae, which was much narrower and also nearer to them. They also sent the fleet to rest near the pass at Artemisium, so that there would be easy communication between the army and the navy, Artemisium, being part of Euboea, where there is a narrow strait to the mainland close to the island of Sciathos.

West of Thermopylae there is a lofty hill which is impossible to climb, and, to the east, the road is shut in by the sea and marshes. The entrance into Greece by means of Trachis is just fifty feet wide and it narrows still further on either side of Thermopylae, just wide enough for a single carriage in some places. There are some hot springs there and an altar devoted to Hercules. The Phocians had raised a protective wall in times gone by to protect themselves from the Thessalians and had also broken up the land with watercourses from the springs. The Greeks repaired the ancient wall and decided to take their stand here against the barbarian, and determined that they could obtain corn from the nearby village of Alpeni. Once they heard of Xerxes' arrival in Pieria, they made haste to their stations.

The Persian fleet now departed from Therma, and ten of the swiftest vessels sailed toward Sciathos, where they gave chase to the three lookout vessels stationed there by the Greeks, one belonging to Troezen, another to Egina, and the third to Athens. The barbarians captured the Troezonian ship and sacrificed the most handsome member of the crew, who was named Leo, and also caught the Eginetan trireme and enslaved the crew, with one exception, called Pythes, who had fought valiantly and to whom they behaved with much kindness. The Athenian ship commanded by Phormus ran itself aground, and the crew made their way back to Athens. The Greek navy heard of this encounter by means of fire signals and abandoned Artemisium for Chalcis, intending to guard the Euripus.

The Persian fleet now came down from Therma to Sepias in Magnesia. The fleet was composed of twelve hundred and seven triremes, each with a crew of two hundred and thirty foot soldiers and three thousand smaller vessels, each manned by, perhaps, eight men. The navy therefore had 517,610 men, and the army 1,700,000 foot soldiers and 80,000 horsemen, with 20,000 Libyan charioteers, giving a total of 2,317,610 men, not counting the camp followers. Such was the force brought from Asia. The Greeks of Thrace added another one hundred and twenty ships to the Persian forces, and foot soldiers were furnished by the Paeonians, Eordians, Bottiaeans, Brygians, Pierians, Macedonians, Perrhaebians, Enianians, Dolopians, Magnesians and Achaeans, perhaps adding 400,000 more men to the Persian army.

As I have said, the Persian fleet was moored on a strip of the Magnesian coast between the city of Casthanaea and Cape Sepias, with the first row of ships moored to the land and the remainder anchored slightly off shore, row upon row, and eight deep. They passed the night uneventfully, but a violent storm blew up at dawn, with a strong gale from the east which the local people call the Hellespontias. Some of the ships succeeded in pulling themselves up onto the shore, but the remainder were caught by the storm and many ships were driven ashore or dashed to pieces. Ameinocles, who farmed an area near Cape Sepias, found gold and silver drinking cups and Persian treasure boxes washed up on the shore and became very wealthy, although he suffered the calamity of losing his offspring. The storm lasted three days, and at least four hundred triremes and uncounted support craft were lost, and the Persians raised a protective barricade around their beached ships lest they be attacked by the Thessalians.

After the storm, the Greek fleet gave thanks to Poseidon and moved back to Artemisium, whereas the Persians proceeded to the bay near Pagasae, where Hercules is said to have been put ashore by Jason and his companions before they deserted him on their voyage to Colchis in search of the Golden Fleece. Fifteen of the Persian ships mistook the fleet at Artemisium for their own and the crew were easily captured and questioned before being sent off in chains.

Xerxes brought the land army down through Thessaly and on to Alus in Achaea into Malis, along the shores of a bay, past the cities of Anticyra and Trachis, where Xerxes pitched his camp. South of Trachis is the Phoenix, a small river, and it is just fifteen furlongs from here to Thermopylae through the village of Anthela. Thus, the two armies took their stand: one the master of all to the north of Trachis, and the other master of the continent to the south.

THERMOPYLAE

The Greek army waiting at Thermopylae was composed of three hundred men at arms from Sparta, five hundred Tegeans and five hundred Mantineans from Arcadia, one hundred and twenty Orchomenians, four hundred from Corinth, two hundred from Phlius, and eighty from Mycenae. There were seven hundred Thespians and four hundred Thebans from Boeotia and one thousand Phocians. In addition, all of the men of Locris were encouraged by envoys from the Greeks who had announced that this was just the vanguard of the main host, to allay any fears of defeat, for the rest of the Greek army could be expected any day and the sea was in the safe keeping of the navy.

The commander of the entire force was Leonidas the Lacedaemonian, who was descended from Hercules over nineteen generations and who had become a King of Sparta unexpectedly after the death of his elder brothers, Dorieus and Cleomenes. Leonidas had handpicked his men, choosing only those who were fathers, as he understood the desperate nature of their task and did not want to cause any families to die out.

The Greeks had taken troops from Thebes, although they suspected that the Thebans really supported the Medes and might not be loyal. The Spartans were sent in front of the main body of the army to encourage the allies to fight and resist the Medes, whereas the main body of the Spartan army was to follow after the end of the Carneian festival. The remainder of the Greek army was also to follow after the Olympic festival, and none expected the contest at Thermopylae to begin so speedily.

Once the Persian host had been drawn up at Thermopylae, the Greeks conferred, and many were in favour of retreating to the isthmus to protect the

Peloponnese. Once Leonidas saw the concern of the local Phocians and Locrians, he decided that they would protect the pass and sent envoys to several cities for help, as they were too few to stand against the Medes.

Xerxes sent a mounted spy to observe the Greeks. He was able to view some of the force unmolested, and it happened that the Lacedaemonians had the watch on the outer wall and were engaged in gymnastics and combing their long hair. The spy reported this to Xerxes, who called upon Demaratus for an explanation and was told: 'I have said to you, sire, how brave were the Lacedaemonians, for they mean to dispute the pass with us, and this is how they prepare themselves for battle. Be assured that if you can subdue the Lacedaemonians here and those that remain in the Peloponnese, then you will win the whole of Greece'.

Xerxes was not convinced, for he wondered how such a small force could face the whole Persian army, and he waited four days before sending the Medes and the Cissians against them on the fifth day with orders to bring them alive into his presence. The Persian forces suffered terrible losses, and it became clear that, although the Persians had many combatants, there was a shortage of true warriors.

As a result, Xerxes sent in the ten thousand but things went on as before, with the armies fighting in a narrow space and the barbarians using shorter spears than those of the Greeks, who also deployed skilful tactics, often turning their backs in flight and then wheeling round to face their pursuers, thus destroying large numbers of the enemy. Xerxes thrice leapt from his throne in terror for his army during the day, and although some Spartans fell, the Persians could not prevail, whether they fought in divisions or in any other way.

The Persians tried again the next day, expecting the Greeks to be weakened by wounds, but the forces of each city took it in turns to defend the pass, each taking the brunt of the battle in turn, save the Phocians who were stationed on the mountain to guard the pathway. Xerxes had made no headway in two days of fighting and was wondering what to do, when a man called Ephialtes came to him in expectation of great reward with information about a mountain path leading to Thermopylae. A price was later put on the head of Ephialtes by the Lacedaemonians, and he fled from Thessaly to Anticyra, where he was slain long afterwards by Athenades, who received the reward despite the fact that he had not killed Ephialtes because of his treachery.

Xerxes was overjoyed and sent the ten thousand along the path with Ephialtes as their guide. The path follows the stream of the Asopus, through a cleft in the hills and along the ridge of the mountain to the city of Alpenus. The Persians continued their march through the whole of the night, keeping the mountains of Oeta on their right and Trachis on their left, until, at dawn, they found themselves close to the summit and challenged by the force of one thousand Phocians stationed there. The mountainside had many groves of oak trees, and the Phocians had heard the rustling of the leaves as the Persians ascended but had not attacked, thinking that they might be Lacedaemonians. Hydarnes, the commander of the ten thousand, learned from Ephialtes the nature of the troops he was facing and arrayed his troops for battle, sending showers of arrows onto the Phocians, who, thinking themselves the target of the attack, fled to the crest of the mountain and prepared to fight to the death.

The Persians, however, decided not to delay on account of the Phocians and passed on, descending the mountain with all possible speed. The Greeks understood from their scouts what had happened and held a conference before dawn and decided that some of the forces would retreat and some would remain with the Spartans to fight to the last. Megistias, a seer who had carried out many sacrifices, decided to stay with the army, although bidden to depart, but sent his son away. Some say that Leonidas himself sent some of the troops away in regard for their safety, but I think that he perceived some of the allies unwilling to face the danger and sent them away knowing that if he stayed, glory awaited him. He also knew of a message from the Oracle that said: 'Either Sparta must be overthrown or one of her Kings must perish'.

Now only the Thespians and the Thebans remained with Leonidas, and the Thebans very much against their will. At dawn, the Persians made libations and began to advance, and the Spartans came out further into the more open part of the pass and brought slaughter to the barbarians, who fell in heaps. The Persian captains whipped their men forwards, and many were thrust into the sea or trampled, for the Greeks knew that the mountain had been crossed and their destruction was at hand and fought with furious valour, reckless of their own safety.

By now their spears had been thrown and the Spartans hewed down the ranks of the Persians with their swords until, eventually, Leonidas fell, together with many famous Spartans whose names I have taken care to record. Many illustrious Persians also fell, including two sons of Darius, Abrocomes and Hyperanthes. A fierce struggle now arose over the ownership of the body of Leonidas, and the Greeks had to drive the Persians back four times before they managed to bear it off. The Greeks now drew into the narrowest part of the pass, behind the wall on a hillock, where they gathered together in one body, with the exception of the Thebans. Here they defended themselves to the last, with those without swords using their hands and teeth until the barbarians had pulled down the wall and surrounded them on all sides and buried them with a hail of missiles.

One of the Trachinians remarked that 'such was the number of barbarians that, when they shot their arrows forth the power of the sun would be weakened by their multitude', and Dieneces the Spartan was heard to say at this time that 'if the Medes darken the sun at least we can now fight in the shade'. Alpheus and Maro and a Thespian called Dithyrambus were also noted for their great valour at this time.

Two of the Spartans previously had a disease of the eyes and had retired to Alpeni but one of them, Eurytus, called for his armour when he heard that the Persians had come around the mountain and had his helot slave lead him to rejoin the battle, where he perished. The other, Aristodemus, returned to Sparta, but no one would give him a light to kindle his fire or say a word to him, although he did wipe away his shame at the battle of Platea. Another man, called Pantites, survived the battle but found such shame when he returned to Sparta that he killed himself.

The Thebans had moved away from the Greeks, when they saw them retire to the hillock for the final stand and gave themselves up to the Persians, saying that they had been forced to fight. Some were slain by the barbarians, and the remainder were branded with the royal mark at the command of Xerxes.

Xerxes now called for another talk with Demaratus, for everything he had said had come to pass. 'How many of the Lacedaemonians are left, and how many are brave warriors such as these?' he asked, and Demaratus replied that 'their numbers are great and they inhabit many cities, but there is a town in Lacedaemonia called Sparta, with eight thousand grown men, each equal to those who have fought here. The others are brave but not such warriors as these'. 'What do you advise, Demaratus, for you were once their King?' asked Xerxes. Demaratus advised: 'Sire, assign three hundred ships to attack the island of Cythera on the shores of Laconia, for once you threaten the Spartans so close to home, they will cease to aid the Greeks and you will subdue Greece, and Sparta, by herself, will be powerless. Otherwise you will find the Greek army massed at the isthmus which leads to the Peloponnese and you will have to fight a far bloodier battle than any you have yet witnessed'.

The King's brother, Achaemenes, counselled him not to listen to Demaratus, saying that the latter was envious of the Persians and sought to ruin them. They had already lost four hundred ships, and, rather than send away another three hundred, he advised that Xerxes keep the army and navy together and not preoccupy himself with what the enemy would do, but order the affairs of his own army and navy appropriately, to guarantee victory. Xerxes took this counsel but advised Achaemenes that he still valued the opinions of Demaratus and would not hear ill spoken of him.

Xerxes now passed through the plain of Thermopylae and ordered the head of Leonidas struck from his body and the body placed upon a cross, showing how angry he was with the state of affairs, for the Persians usually honour valiant warriors.

I want to return to an item not yet mentioned, which is how the Lacedaemonians first heard of the plans for the Persians to invade Greece. Demaratus must have had no great desire to help the Lacedaemonians, and so I am not sure whether he sent the message through good will or insolent triumph, but he scraped the wax from some tablets and wrote the message upon the wood and then covered the tablets up with wax again before sending the message on to Sparta where Gorgo, the wife of Leonidas, understood how to read it. The Greeks were thus appraised of the Persian intent to invade Greece.

ARTEMISIUM

The Greek navy was under the command of a Lacedaemonian called Eurybiades, for the allies had said that they would never serve under an Athenian, even though the Athenians had supplied the most ships. The Athenians did not press their claim for command because they knew that a quarrel would bring Greece to ruin.

The Greek navy consisted of two hundred and seventy-one ships, not including the penteconters, with one hundred and twenty-seven from Athens, eighteen from the Eginetans, twelve from the Sicyonians, ten from the Lacedaemonians, eight from the Epidaurians, and two from the Styreans, along with the Ceans, who provided two triremes and two penteconters.

The Greek fleet arrived at Artemisium, but Eurybiades became distressed on seeing the barbarian ships at anchor near Aphetae and was for withdrawing. The Euboeans were eager to remove their women and children from the area and appealed for him to wait a few days. When they saw that they had failed to persuade him, they went to Themistocles and bribed him with thirty talents on his promise that the fleet would stay and fight in defence of Euboea.

Themistocles handed over five talents to Eurybiades, pretending that they had come from his own pocket, and said to the Corinthian commander, who was the only remaining voice of opposition, that he would pay him more for remaining loyal than the Medes could pay him for a betrayal and sent three talents of silver. So Themistocles was able to keep his promise to the Euboeans and make a profit, as everyone thought that the money had been provided by Athens.

Meanwhile the Persians had seen that the Greek fleet was weak in numbers and sent two hundred ships around the island of Sciathos in the hope of encircling the whole fleet and scoring a decisive victory, while the rest of the fleet waited at Aphetae. The Persians had a skilful diver called Scyllias, who had been looking for an opportunity to defect to the Greeks. He chose this time to dive into the sea and, they say, he did not surface for a full eighty furlongs and came over to the Greeks to share information on the Persian plan of attack and on their losses in the storm.

The Greeks now planned to sail out after midnight and meet with the two hundred ships, but, as the day wore on, they resolved to wait until the evening and attack the main body of the Persian fleet directly, so that they could gauge their mettle. The Persian commanders thought that the Greeks were mad in attacking them with such a small number of ships and decided to surround the vessels sailing toward them. On a signal, the Greek ships came together in the shape of a compass, with their sterns together and their prows facing outward, and thus managed to capture thirty Persian ships before nightfall, after which the Greeks sailed back to Artemisium and the Persians to Aphetae.

That midsummer evening ended with heavy rain and a storm which washed the corpses and broken pieces of the ships from the battle onto the oars of the Persian ships at Aphetae, depressing them considerably. The two hundred Persian ships sailing around to prepare an ambush were caught by the storm in the Hollows of

Euboea, and the squadron was entirely lost. The next morning the Greeks were reinforced, with fifty-three ships arriving from Athens, and the two navies were now more evenly matched. The Greeks sailed out again toward the Persian fleet, capturing some Cilician ships before retiring to Artemisium.

These happened to be the same days as those on which the fighting at Thermopylae had taken place, and the Greeks were defending the pass and the Euripus at the same time. On the third day, the Persian captains advanced toward the Greek fleet, ashamed that such a small number of ships had caused them such trouble, and afraid of the anger of Xerxes. The Persians approached Artemisium in a great semi-circle, hoping to entrap all of the Greeks, and a great sea battle ensued, with losses on both sides, with the Egyptians showing great valour by capturing five vessels from the Greeks. The Athenians had also fought bravely, but half of their ships were damaged and they determined to break from their station when both sides had retired at the end of the day.

Themistocles gave orders to the soldiers to slaughter the Euboean cattle, and then the news arrived of the fate of Leonidas at Thermopylae. The Greek fleet immediately left Artemisium, and Themistocles sent his swiftest ships to carve inscriptions on the rocks at every naval watering hole and port in an attempt to make the Greeks fighting for the Persians come over to his side. The inscriptions read: 'Men of Ionia. You are wrong to help your enemy to enslave Greece. We beseech you to come over to our side or refrain from combat. If you are forced to oppose us, then consider fighting backwardly, remembering that you fight your own brothers'.

Xerxes had left just one thousand of the twenty thousand Persian dead at Thermopylae on the field and buried the remainder in trenches hidden from view before collecting his forces at Histiaea and inviting them to view the battlefield where the four thousand bodies of the fallen Greeks were displayed. The next day the army continued the march toward Athens.

THE SACK OF ATHENS

The Persian army now marched from Thessaly into the land of the Phocians, guided by the Thessalians, who had, a few years before, been at war with the Phocians and were still on bad terms with them. Indeed, I think it likely that if the Thessalians had decided to fight for Greece, then the Phocians might well have sent earth and water to the Persians.

The Thessalians had previously attacked the Phocians with full force, and the latter had retreated up the mountain of Parnassus and blockaded themselves. In the middle of the night, the Phocians had selected six hundred of their best warriors and covered them in chalk dust and attacked the Thessalian camp with orders to kill anyone not daubed in white like themselves. The Thessalians took fright and thought that demons were amongst them and, by means of this ruse, the Phocians succeeded in killing four thousand men. The Phocians had also dealt a blow to the Thessalian cavalry by digging a great pit at a pass near the city of Hyampolis and filling it with empty wine jars, and then covering the ground with earth again. The Thessalian cavalry saw the Phocian forces and charged at full speed to attack, but became entangled in the wine jars which broke the legs of all the horses.

The Thessalians, who had quarrelled with the Phocians, now sent them a messenger, demanding a payment of fifty talents of silver or they would use their influence with the barbarians to ensure that the entire

Phocian nation was enslaved. The Phocians replied that they would not pay any amount to the Thessalians, for they could offer earth and water to the King on their own account if necessary and, in any case, they would not betray the cause of the Greeks.

As a result, the Thessalians led the Persian army through the land of the Phocians. Many of the people had taken refuge in the mountains of Parnassus, particularly at Tithorea, near the city of Neon, which could shelter a large body of men. Others had fled to the city of Amphissa above the Crissaean plain. The army marched along the valley of the Cephissus, burning the towns of Drymus, Charadra, Erochus, Tethronium, Amphicaea, Neon, Pedieis, Triteis, Elateia, Hyampolis, Parapotamii and Abae along the way. There was an Oracle at Abae, as there is today, and the Persians plundered and burnt the temple and killed a number of Phocians and caused the death of some of their women.

The army marched on to Panopeis and split into two, with Xerxes taking the larger part of the force on toward Athens and the other part marching toward Delphi, laying waste to parts of Phocis as they passed through. The Delphians heard that the Persians were approaching and consulted the Oracle, which advised them that the gods would take care of the temple and that they should flee. Flee they did, some up to Parnassus and others to the Corycian cave sacred to Pan, with one faction joining the Phocians in the city of Amphissa in Locris.

The barbarians drew close to the temple and were keen to regard the riches, for they had heard of the many gifts to the Oracle, including those given by Croesus. As they approached the temple of Athena Pronaia, the sacred armour was seen lying outside the temple, and a storm burst over their heads and two crags split off from Mount Parnassus and fell on them, crushing large numbers, while a war cry of victory was heard from the temple. The barbarians were terrified and turned and fled, and the Delphians saw this and came out of their hiding places to slay the enemy, and two armed warriors, larger than human, were seen pursuing and slaying the army as they fled, and thus the Persian force was forced to retire from the temple. The Delphians maintain that the two warriors were two heroes, Phylacus and Autonous, whose shrines lay nearby.

The Athenians were dismayed that no attempt had been made to stop the Persian army in Boeotia, and so the Greek navy proceeded to Salamis at the request of the Athenians and a proclamation was issued in Athens that each citizen should save his household and children as best they could. The Athenians say that there is a huge serpent living in the acropolis who is guardian of the whole place and that they feed it honey cake each month. The priestess announced that the food had not been eaten and that the snake had abandoned the city, and so the Athenian ships took the families to Egina and Salamis or, for the most part, to Troezen, and Athens was abandoned.

Eurybiades was the commander of the Greek navy, which was now stationed at the port of the Troezenians, and there were a greater number of ships than had fought at Artemisium, now totalling three hundred and seventy-eight triremes, of which one hundred and eighty were from Athens. The captains were in conference, deciding perhaps to give battle to the Persians in defence of the Peloponnese, when news came that the Persian army was laying waste to Athens and had burnt Thespiae and Plataea on its march through Boeotia.

Four months had gone by since the Persian army had crossed the Hellespont, and they found Athens forsaken and abandoned, with very few people remaining in the city. Some Athenians had fortified the citadel with planks and boards, imagining this to be the wooden wall that the Oracle had predicted would protect them. The Persians encamped on the hill opposite and began shooting fire arrows and succeeded in burning the wooden rampart. A path up to the citadel was eventually found, and the Persians climbed up and rushed to the gates, slew the remaining Athenians and plundered the temple and burnt every part of the citadel.

Xerxes was now the master of Athens and dispatched a message to Artabanus in Susa informing him of his success.

SALAMIS

As soon as the captains of the fleet heard of the sack of Athens, they voted that they should give battle to the Persians at the Isthmus and depart from Salamis. An Athenian called Mnesiphilus approached Themistocles and pointed out that: 'if these men sail away from Salamis, they will scatter back to their own homes and Greece will be ruined'.

Themistocles therefore went to Eurybiades and bade him reconvene the council of captains so that they could reconsider. At the meeting he made no mention of the fleet scattering and begged Eurybiades directly: 'O Eurybiades! It is in your power to save Greece as you consider between two courses. If you fight at the Isthmus you will be in open waters, which is to our disadvantage, as our ships are fewer and heavier than the enemy's and you will have already lost Salamis, Megara and Egina, even if all goes well for us. If we fight here in narrow waters, Salamis may be preserved and we will send the enemy away in disorder and save the Peloponnese just as well as if we had fought at the Isthmus'.

Adeimantus the Corinthian now attacked Themistocles and challenged his right to speak, for now that Athens was in the hands of the barbarians, Themistocles did not represent any Greek city and should have no voice. Themistocles reminded the captains that, with two hundred ships and many men at his command, he had both city and territory as good as anyone else and that: 'if we stay here and fight then all will be well, otherwise we will take our ships and our families and leave for our colony, Siris, in Italy and you will rue the day when you lost us as allies'. Eurybiades now made his decision to stay and fight at Salamis, for he could not very well proceed without the Athenians.

The Persian army was now more numerous than before, for it had picked up troops from the Malians, the Locrians, the Boeotians and some of the Dorians, excepting those peoples who had fought on the side of the Greeks. The fleet was anchored at Phalerum, the port of Athens, and Xerxes now held a conference to determine whether to attack the Grecian fleet at Salamis or press on to the Peloponnese.

All of the assembled captains advised that they engage the Greeks, with the exception of Queen Artemisia, who warned: 'Spare thy ships and do not risk a battle with these skilful sailors. Instead, march your army, with the fleet attending close by, on toward the Peloponnese and you will easily achieve the conquest of Greece, for they cannot hold out against you for very long and surely they will not trouble themselves to battle very hard on behalf of the Athenians. On the other hand, if you fight this sea battle and lose, then I worry for the safety of your land army'.

Xerxes was pleased with her advice but nevertheless ordered the sea battle, for he thought that the fleet had not done its best at Euboea and would fight much better with their King watching the outcome of the battle. The land army was dispatched toward the Peloponnese, where the Greeks had been making preparations since the fall of Leonidas by blocking up the Scironian Way, and tens of thousands of people had begun building a barricade across the Isthmus. Not all of the nations of the Peloponnese had given their aid, and the Lacedaemonians, Arcadians, Eleans, Corinthians, Scironians, Epidaurians, Phliasians, Troezenians and Hermionians were all alarmed at the danger facing Greece, whereas the remaining nations by their inaction were taking the side of the Medes.

The Greek captains at Salamis began to mutter about the merits of defending a land that had already been conquered and were again moving toward the idea of defending the Peloponnese. Seeing this, Themistocles took matters into his own hands and instructed his slave, Sicinnus, to give a message to the Persian commanders that the Greeks were considering fleeing from Salamis forthwith. Overnight the Persians took action, moving their ships from Ceos and Cynosura to blockade the strait to Munychia and landing a force of men on the island of Psyttaleia, which lay between Salamis and the mainland, so that any ships and crew washed up there during the battle might be dealt with. All of this was done without the knowledge of the Greeks.

The Greek captains were still considering their course of action when Aristides arrived by boat, having crossed from Egina. Aristides had been ostracised from Athens and was not a friend of Themistocles, but he put aside his enmity and, after talking with Themistocles, addressed the captains and informed them that the barbarians had blockaded Salamis, and that his ship had only just managed to slip through. The captains still doubted, but a Tenian trireme defected from the Persians and confirmed that the fleet was, indeed, surrounded, and at dawn speeches were made to the men and the ships readied for battle.

The Greek fleet was attacked as soon as it left land, and the ships began to backwater, when, it is said, a phantom in the form of a woman appeared to the whole fleet and urged them to fight. An Athenian captain, Ameinias, charged his ship forwards, where it became entangled with a vessel of the enemy. The Phoenician ships had been lined up against the Athenians, and the Ionians against the Lacedaemonians, and only a few of the Ionians had heeded Themistocles' plea to fight backwardly. The Persian forces fought more bravely than at Euboea, perhaps through fear, as the eyes of Xerxes were upon them, but the Greeks fought in order and kept their line, whereas the Persian ships were in confusion and a much larger number of Persian ships were disabled.

I do not have detailed information on the battle but I know that Artemisia's ship was pursued by an Athenian trireme and she had nowhere to fly to, for there were friendly ships all around her. She chose to bear down on one of their own ships, which was carrying the Calyndian King, causing it to sink with the loss of all the crew. I do not know if she had a dispute with this crew, but it worked to her advantage because the Athenian captain thought that she was now fighting on the Greek side and gave up the chase. He cannot have recognised her ship because the Athenians had special orders regarding Artemisia and a ten thousand drachma reward for her capture, as they were indignant that a woman should appear against them. Xerxes was watching the battle, and Artemisia was pointed out to him as having sunk an enemy ship and, as nobody survived to dispute this, Artemisia was doubly fortunate, leading Xerxes to comment that 'my men have behaved like women and my women like men'.

One of the chief commanders of the Persian fleet, a son of Darius called Ariabignes, was killed, along with a vast number of high-ranking Persians: Greek losses were much less severe because all of the Greek sailors could swim, and made their way toward Salamis, whereas the Persians could not, and drowned. Many of the Persian ships to the rear were pressing forward and became entangled with the ships in front which were trying to back away from the Greeks.

Xerxes sat on a hill called Aegaleos, overlooking Salamis, for the whole battle, making sure that the name of any captain performing worthy exploits was recorded. A deputation of Phoenicians whose ships had been sunk made an appearance before him at this time and accused the Ionians of wilfully destroying their vessels and acting as traitors. Fortunately for the Ionians, at that moment Xerxes was able to observe an Eginetan ship crippling a Samothracian ship whose crew responded by using javelins to clear the decks of their attackers, allowing them to come aboard and take the Greek ship. This saved the reputation of the Ionians, and Xerxes had the deputation of Phoenicians beheaded to prevent them, he said, from ever blaming other men for their own misconduct.

The rout of the barbarians eventually began, and the Persian ships tried to escape to Phalerum but were met by the Eginetan fleet, whereas any that fled to the shore were dealt with by the Athenians. Aristides, an Athenian, landed troops on the islet of Psyttaleia to deal with the Persians there. Indeed, firstly the Eginetans, and then the Athenians, gained the greater glory in this battle. The Athenians say that the Corinthians sailed away at the beginning of the battle and only turned about and joined in once the battle had been won, although the Corinthians say that they fought bravely.

The Greeks regrouped after this victory to prepare for another engagement, but Xerxes became alarmed after he saw the extent of his losses and grew fearful that the Greeks would make for the Hellespont and destroy his bridges, and so the battle ended with a great victory for the Greek navy.

THE PERSIANS RETREAT

Xerxes ordered a mound built across the channel to Salamis and had some boats bound together as a bridge, as if he were making preparations to join again in battle with the Greek navy. However, his general, Mardonius, had guessed, from long experience of the King, that Xerxes was now fearful that the Greeks would destroy the bridges at the Hellespont and that his life might be in danger, and that he would soon order a retreat.

A message was sent to Susa carrying news of the defeat to Persia, and nothing goes faster than a Persian messenger, where men and horses are posted a day's journey apart all the length of the route. The Persians had celebrated when they heard that Xerxes was master of Athens, but now they rent their garments and cried in the streets and blamed Mardonius for their defeat and prayed for the safe return of their King.

Mardonius realised that he was likely to be blamed for the misfortunes of the Persian forces and considered that it would be best for him to take command once Xerxes had left and conquer Greece or else die gloriously in battle, and so he addressed Xerxes: 'Master, the Greeks still would not dare attack our land forces, and it is within our power to attack the Peloponnese immediately or perhaps wait awhile if you so desire. If you are thinking of retreat, then please consider that the Persians are not cowards and if you let me choose but 300,000 troops, I can bring all Greece under your power while you return to Persia with the bulk of the army'.

Xerxes felt great joy at this counsel and drew his advisors together to confer with them: 'Mardonius has advised me to stay and attack, for he says that the Persian part of the land forces are not to blame for any of the disasters which have befallen us and he offers an alternative, through which he will remain with 300,000 and enslave Greece while I retire with the rest of the army and return home'. Artemisia gave counsel that 'it would seem right for you to return home, for if Mardonius achieves a victory it would be as your victory achieved by your own slaves, and if he loses it would not be of consequence, for you would be safe and the Greeks would have gained a poor victory and your house will still flourish'.

Xerxes then bade Artemisia and one of his principal eunuchs, Hermotimus, escort certain of his children to Ephesus. Now, Hermotimus had been made a prisoner of war when he was young and ended up in the hands of a certain Panionius, a native of Chios, who made his living by obtaining boys of unusual beauty and making them eunuchs and selling them in Sardis or Ephesus for large sums of money. Hermotimus had suffered so and had been sent from Sardis to the King, where he had become one of the principal eunuchs and valued very highly by Xerxes. Hermotimus happened to chance upon Panionius on the journey to Athens with the Persian army and had a long and friendly talk with him and invited him and his family to Sardis, promising him all sorts of favours. Panionius did not recognise Hermotimus and came with his family to Sardis, whereupon he had Panionius make eunuchs of his own four sons by his own hand, and made his sons treat him in the same way. Thus Hermotimus wreaked his terrible revenge.

XERXES

Xerxes now bade Mardonius choose his army and, as night fell, he issued orders and the fleet left Phalerum and sped toward the Hellespont to protect the bridges. On the following day, the Greeks saw the land forces still encamped and did not realise for a while that the fleet had left. They soon gave chase but got as far as Andros without finding the Persian fleet and held council, where Themistocles urged them to go straight to the Hellespont and destroy the bridge. Eurybiades, however, considered that they should let the Persian forces leave Greece as speedily and as easily as possible for, if they stayed, they might resolve to conquer Greece if only just to prevent themselves from dying of hunger. The council agreed, and Themistocles urged them to return home and tend to their homes and families, but to gather again in the spring and sail to the Hellespont and on to Ionia.

He also sent his slave Sicinnus again to the Persian King with the message that he, Themistocles, had 'rendered him a service by persuading the Greeks not to pursue the fleet or destroy the bridges but to allow the Persians to retreat without harm'. This Themistocles did to guarantee favour from the Persians in case he had trouble in Athens. Themistocles, now that the fleet was no longer giving chase to the Persians, demanded a large sum of money from the people of the island of Andros for his own gain and besieged them when they would not pay. In the same way he received money from the Carystians and the Parians.

The Persian army waited a few days more and then departed back into Boeotia and on to Thessaly, where

Mardonius made his choice of troops, which included the ten thousand and the one thousand royal cavalry, and both foot soldiers and horsemen from the Medes, Sacans, Bactrians and Indians. He also took troops who were of remarkable appearance or known to be valiant to make up the numbers to 300,000.

Xerxes took forty-five days to reach the Hellespont and was unable to recover the sacred chariot and steeds of Zeus that he had left along the road at Siris in Paeonia. His troops suffered greatly from hunger and dysentery, and many died en route, with more dying at Abydos, where large numbers of the hungry ate and drank too much and died from excess. The remainder returned safely to Sardis with Xerxes.

There is a story that Xerxes entrusted his army to Hydarnes and boarded a Phoenician ship to sail to Asia. A storm blew up, and the ship ran into difficulties because of the number of Persian nobles attending on Xerxes, these causing the ship to be overloaded. 'Is there any way that we might escape this danger?' asked Xerxes of the helmsman, who replied: 'There is no way, Master, for there are too many aboard the vessel'. Xerxes called out to the passengers: 'Men of Persia. Now is the time to show your love for your King!', and the Persians immediately bowed to their Lord and jumped overboard. On reaching land, Xerxes rewarded the helmsman with gold for saving his life and then ordered him beheaded for putting him in danger.

PLATAEA

The Greeks met at the Isthmus to make offerings to the gods and divide the spoils, and Eurybiades and Themistocles were given wreaths of olives, although Themistocles was reproached by some of his enemies for taking the glory of the Athenians as his own.

Artabazus accompanied Xerxes safely to Asia with sixty thousand troops and returned to find Mardonius in his winter quarters in Thessaly. The Potidaeans had just revolted, and Artabazus laid siege to them and to the Olynthians, whom he thought were about to revolt. He took their city and led the inhabitants to a marsh, where he had them slain, before handing the city over to the Chalcideans. The Potidaeans resisted the siege for three months until an unusually low tide encouraged the Persians to come along the shore only to be swept away by a very high tide, which drowned all those who could not swim and left the rest to be picked off by the Potidaeans in sailing ships. Thus Artabazus rejoined Mardonius with what was left of his troops.

Mardonius first sent to all the Oracles, including those at Lebadeia, Abae of the Phocians and Thebes, although I do not have a record of the prophecies. He then sent Alexander of Macedon, whose sister was married to a Persian, to the Athenians as an envoy to negotiate a treaty.

Alexander was descended from Perdiccas, who had obtained the kingdom of Macedonia in the following manner. Three brothers fled from Argos to Illyria, where they made themselves useful to the King, one tending the horses, and another to the cows, whereas Perdiccas, the youngest, looked after the smaller cattle. In those days, even the kings were poor and the Queen would bake the bread each day, and she noticed that the bread allocated to Perdiccas would rise to double the size of the others.

The King was superstitious and ordered the brothers to be gone at once when he heard of this miracle. 'What about our pay?' they asked, and, as a reply, the King pointed to a spot of sunlight shining though onto the kitchen floor and said 'Take that as your pay and go!' The brothers looked at each other, and Perdiccas cut around the sun with his knife and said: 'We accept your payment', and they left. The King thought that perhaps there was something in this and sent his guards to kill the brothers, but they had already crossed the river and settled near a mountain called Bermius, from whence they slowly conquered Macedonia.

Alexander made an offer to the Athenians: 'O Men of Athens. Mardonius bids you on behalf of the King to consent to enter into a league with me and your lands will be restored and you will be forgiven for any acts against the Persians and you will live as free men and have your temples restored'.

The Lacedaemonians had also sent envoys to Athens, for they had heard that Mardonius was going to try to bring them onto his side: 'We Lacedaemonians entreat the Athenians not to agree terms with the barbarian. for to do so would be doubly dishonest, for the Persians came here because you sought to extend your empire. It would be intolerable for a nation to which so many owe their freedom to became the means of bringing Greece into slavery. We feel for the loss of your homes and of your harvest for the past two years and offer your womenfolk sustenance for as long as the war endures'.

After a while, the Athenians made their reply to Alexander: 'We cling to freedom in the face of the power of the Mede, for as long as the sun rises we will oppose Xerxes with the help of the gods and heroes whose temples he has burnt', and to the Lacedaemonians they spoke that 'not all the gold in the world would bribe us to help the Medes to enslave the Greeks and we could not come to terms with a nation that has burnt our temples or betray our countrymen with whom we have a common language. Know then that, as long as one Athenian lives, we will oppose Xerxes. We thank you for your wish to give our families sustenance but we can endure. We ask you to lead out your troops and let us give battle in Boeotia before our foe hears our answer and marches here to Attica'.

Mardonius immediately marched out from Thessaly and, sped on by the Thessalians, his forces arrived at Thebes, where the Thebans encouraged him to camp and sent presents to the Greek leaders in the hope of achieving his aims without the need for a battle. Mardonius pushed on and took a deserted Athens for the second time, ten months after the first, with the inhabitants fleeing mainly to Salamis. He sent an envoy again to the Athenians at Salamis, offering terms, and a citizen called Lycidas urged for the proposal to be put to the people, but he was stoned to death and the womenfolk went to his house and stoned his family also, thus ending any possibility of agreement.

The Lacedaemonians were keeping the feast of Hyacinthia, and the Athenians were angry because they had not furnished troops to attack the Persian army in Boeotia as requested but had been busy completing the wall across the Isthmus. Now envoys were sent requesting troops so that they could fight the Persians in Attica, perhaps on the plain of Thria. The Lacedaemonians procrastinated for ten days and gave no answer and finally ordered five thousand troops to march from the Isthmus under the command of Pausanias against the 'strangers', which is the name they give to the barbarians.

The Ephors also sent their troops, and a further five thousand men, accompanied by their Helots, set off from Sparta. The Argives had agreed with the Persians to stop any troops passing through their territory but refrained from combat and sent messages to Mardonius that they were too weak to oppose the forces marching to Attica. Mardonius had, so far, not laid waste to Attica but, on hearing that the Spartans were coming, and realising that his negotiations were fruitless, he burned Athens and marched for Thebes, for Attica was not good country for fighting on horseback.

His army camped along the Asopus, stretched from Erythrae to Hysiae, in an area in which he had already chopped down the trees, and he ordered a wooden rampart ten furlongs built on each side to make a refuge for his army. I have heard from Thersander that, at this time, the Thebans held a feast for fifty Persians and fifty Thebans who sat together drinking and eating, and at one point a Persian wept as he declared that in a few days most of his number would have been killed.

The Phocians had sent a thousand troops to Mardonius, for they had been compelled to do so, and took up a position on the plain away from the main army. A rumour started that the Persians were bent on destroying them, and they found themselves surrounded by Persian cavalry, whereupon they closed ranks and the cavalry were unable to attack, if indeed they had been planning to do so. Mardonius sent a herald to them: 'Fear not Phocians, I was testing your valour and find you worthy to fight alongside us'.

The Lacedaemonians now marched out from the Isthmus in one force and joined with the Athenians at Eleusis and on into Boeotia, where they camped facing the enemy on the slopes of Mount Cithaeron. Mardonius saw that they could not be enticed out into the plain and sent his cavalry, fighting in divisions under the command of Masistius, to harass them, which they did successfully, causing much damage and insulting the Greeks by calling them women.

One area defended by the Megarians was under particular pressure, and Pausanias asked for volunteers to replace the troops here who were flagging, and a band of three hundred Athenians commanded by Olympiodorus took their place. It happened that an arrow hit the horse ridden by Masistius during one of these attacks and threw the rider. The Athenians rushed him but were not able to take his life, for he resisted and had a breastplate of golden scales until one of the soldiers drew his weapon into his eye and killed him. The Persian cavalry missed their commander and then formed all their divisions into one line to attack and recover the body, but they were repulsed when reinforcements arrived from the remaining Greeks and after some time decided to return to Mardonius for further orders.

Masistius was second only to Mardonius in prestige among the Persians, and the whole Persian army expressed their grief by lamenting and shaving their heads and cutting the manes of their horses and pack animals, thus honouring their dead commander. The Greeks now gained high levels of morale and paraded the dead body of Masistius along the ranks of the army, for the body was of great stature and beauty. The Greeks removed themselves close to the fountain of Gargaphia, in the sacred precinct of the hero Androcrates, in the plain of Plataea.

The Lacedaemonians held one wing, and the Tegeans and the Athenians began to argue over who would have the privilege of the other, citing ancient battles and deeds to determine which nation should have the right. The Athenians eventually urged the Tegeans to 'put aside ancient rites, for a nation brave in the past may have become cowardly and we have as great a record as any other nation. If we just take the battle of Marathon, where we fought alone against the Persians, you will see that we deserve the honour. However, we are happy to comply with the wishes of our commander and let the Lacedaemonians decide where we shall fight'.

The Greek army was deployed thus: Ten thousand Lacedaemonians held the right wing, of which five thousand were Spartans, attended by thirty-five thousand Helots, who were lightly armed, with seven Helots for each Spartan warrior. Fifteen hundred Tegeans held a place of honour next to the Spartans, for they were courageous fighters. Then came five thousand Corinthians and a small band of three hundred from Potidaea in Phocis. Then six hundred from Orchomenus, three thousand Sicyonians, eight hundred Epidaurians, one thousand Troezenians, two hundred Lepreats, four hundred Mycenaeans and Tirynthians, one thousand Phliasians, three hundred Hermionians, six hundred Eretrians and Styreans, four hundred Chalcideans and five hundred Ambraciots. After these came eight hundred Leucadians and Anactorians, two hundred Cephallenians, five hundred Eginetans, three thousand Megarians and six hundred Plataeans. Finally, eight thousand Athenians occupied the left wing under Aristides.

All of the troops, with the exception of the Helots, were heavily armed, making a total of thirty-eight thousand, seven hundred men, with thirty-five thousand lightly armed Helots accompanying the Spartans and thirty-four thousand, five hundred other lightly armed troops belonging to the other Lacedaemonians and Greeks, at a ratio of one lightly armed to every heavily armed warrior. Eighteen hundred was all that was left of the Thespians after Thermopylae, and this brought the total number of men in the Greek army to one hundred and ten thousand.

Mardonius drew up his forces and deepened the ranks and put the Persian soldiers against the Lacedaemonians, with the others facing the Tegeans, on the advice of the Thebans. Next the Medes faced the Corinthians and Potidaeans and so forth, then the Indians, then the Sacans, and, finally, the Boeotians, Locrians, Malians, Thessalians, and the one thousand Phocians facing the Athenians, Plataeans and Megarians, although not all of the Phocians had joined Mardonius and several bands had been harassing them. Mixed in with the Persian troops were many from differing nations such as the Phrygians, Thracians, Paeonians and Ethiopians, but the Egyptians had all left with Xerxes. The Persian forces numbered 300,000, as I have already said, fortified with perhaps 50,000 additional Greek forces who had made alliances with Mardonius.

The next day, both armies made their sacrifices. The Greek sacrifices were made by Tisamenus, who was one of the few Greeks to have been given Lacedaemonian citizenship, for it was prophesied that he would help to win five major battles for the Spartans. Tisamenus found the victims favourable if the Greeks stayed on the defensive but not if they began the battle or crossed the Asopus. Hegesistratus was the soothsayer for the Persians and also found that the Persians should stay on the defensive and not begin the attack. Hegesistratus had once been taken captive by the Spartans and had cut off his own leg and left it in the stocks, while he escaped and lived to tell the tale and made himself a wooden foot and an enemy of Sparta. So he offered the sacrifice with a good will, particularly as he was well paid, and because of his hatred of the Spartans.

The armies squared up to each other for eight days, with neither wanting to start the fight. Mardonius sent his cavalry up to the slopes of Mount Cithaeron to stop the fresh troops who were arriving to support the Greek side and immediately managed to destroy or carry off a supply caravan of some five hundred beasts. Another two days passed, with Mardonius advancing as far as the Asopus to tempt the Greeks over, with the Persian cavalry harassing the Greeks constantly urged on by the Thebans. Mardonius finally grew impatient with the number of Greeks swelling the ranks each day and called a conference on the eleventh day. Artabazus thought it best to break and retreat to the fortifications of the town of Thebes, where they had abundant supplies and where they could use the time to spread some gold amongst the Greeks until their zeal for battle was diminished. The Thebans agreed with Artabazus, but Mardonius was keen for battle, as their army was superior and, as each day passed, the Greeks received more reinforcements.

Mardonius called all his captains together, asking if any knew of any prophesies which said that the Persians would be destroyed in Greece. Nobody answered, and so Mardonius spoke: 'There is a prophecy which says that the Persian army will be destroyed if we should sack the temple of Delphi: however, we have not sacked the temple, and nor will we attempt to do so in the future, so you can rest assured that we will not be destroyed and we will get the better of the Greeks in battle'. Thus, Mardonius made his decision, and Alexander of Macedon was able to get away for a while to the Greek lines and pass on this intelligence, to stand him in good stead if the Greeks won, along with the information that Mardonius had only a few days' supplies left in his stores.

Pausanias considered the intelligence that the fight would probably begin in the morning and decided to switch the wings around because the Athenians had already fought the Medes and were familiar with the fighting tactics of the Persians, whereas the Spartans, who had never fought the Medes, would be better positioned against the Greek forces fighting on the Persian side. The Athenians agreed, and the troops exchanged wings, but this was perceived by the Boeotians, and Mardonius at once redeployed his forces accordingly, and so Pausanias tried to switch his wings once more, to be followed again by Mardonius doing the same.

Mardonius sent a herald to the Lacedaemonians 'We have been told that you Lacedaemonians are the bravest of warriors and that you never turn your backs nor quit your ranks in a fight but always stand firm and either die at your posts or destroy your enemy. Yet we see you fleeing from us before battle has even started, leaving the Athenians to fight us while you set yourselves against our slaves. We expected you to challenge us and offer to fight the Persians by yourselves, and, as no such challenge has come, we send one to you. Choose a number of men and fight against the same number of Persians and let the outcome decide the battle for both armies.'

Mardonius received no reply to his challenge and was elated by this empty victory and sent out the cavalry to attack the Greek line. The cavalry kept their distance, for they had javelins and bows, and caused the Greeks considerable distress. The fountain of Gargaphia had, by now, become choked, and the cavalry prevented the Greeks from obtaining water from the river Asopus and fresh provisions were also prevented from coming through. The Greeks held a council and decided that if the Persians did not attack that day, they would move to a spot of land about ten furlongs away where the river flowed on either side, so that they could have water and the cavalry would not be able to harass them.

AMOMPHARETUS

The Greeks suffered all day and struck camp at nightfall, but the first of these troops marched to the temple of Hera outside the town of Plataea, rather than the agreed destination. Pausanias ordered the Lacedaemonians to follow, but one of their captains, Amompharetus, who had not been at the meeting of the captains that afternoon, refused to move, saying that he 'would not fly from the strangers, nor bring disgrace upon Sparta'. While Pausanias and the other commanders were arguing with Amompharetus, the Athenians sent a messenger because they were waiting for the Spartans to march before they left their post, knowing that sometimes the Spartans said one thing and did another. The Athenian messenger found them still arguing, with Amompharetus heaving a great boulder and leaving it at the feet of Pausanias, saying: 'with this pebble I vote not to abandon our posts and flee from the strangers'.

Finally, at dawn, Pausanias gave the order for the retreat, and the Lacedaemonians retreated along the line of the hills, whereas the Athenians retreated along the hilly ground around Mount Cithaeron to avoid trouble with the Persian cavalry. After a while, Amompharetus decided to follow the main force at a walk and he finally rejoined it at the temple of Demeter at Argiopius, on the river Moloeis, when the whole force of the Persian cavalry attacked them.

Mardonius now crossed the Asopus with his Persian troops and gave chase to the Lacedaemonians and Tegeans only, but he could not see that the Athenians had separated, and the remaining barbarians crossed the river in disorder and gave chase, thinking that the Greeks were running away. The Spartans sent a messenger to the Athenians, appealing for reinforcements, as they were under attack and asked that, if the Athenians themselves were sorely vexed, they might at least send some archers, but the latter were under attack from the Greeks on the barbarian side and could not offer assistance.

The Spartans quickly made their sacrifices, but the victims were not good and the Persians made a wall of their wicker shields and were raining arrows down on the 50,000 Lacedaemonians and the 3,000 Tegeans, until, finally, the Tegeans rushed forward, followed by the Spartans, and a fierce fight occurred until the wicker wall was breached and a hand-to-hand struggle ensued. The Persians were as brave as the Greeks but they were lightly armed without bucklers and not as well trained for such combat, and they dashed forward onto the Spartan ranks in small groups and perished. However, the fight went well for the Persians, led by Mardonius, mounted on a white horse and surrounded by a thousand hand-picked men. When Mardonius fell, the Persian troops took flight in disorder toward the wooden defence which they had raised on Theban territory.

Meanwhile, Artabazus had led his 40,000 troops into battle in an orderly array but at a slow pace, and when he saw the rest of the Persian forces in flight from the Lacedaemonians, he turned his troops around and marched them past Thebes, heading for the Hellespont at all possible speed.

Most of the Greeks on the Persian side fought in a cowardly fashion, except for the Boeotians and Thebans, who fought well against the Athenians but were eventually routed and fled in a different direction from that of the Persian force and carried on into Thebes. The non-Persian troops fled without joining battle as soon as the Persians began to retreat, and so the entire army fled, although the Persian and Boeotian cavalry did good service in protecting their own fugitives from the Greeks, who pressed on and slew the remainder of the army.

The Lacedaemonians reached the wooden fortress of the Persians first but were unable to make any headway because they were unskilled in the art of attacking walled places and they had to wait for the Athenians before the wooden wall could be breached. The Tegeans were the first to break into the fortress, where they plundered the tent of Mardonius, and resistance seemed to fall away and the Persians were easily slaughtered by the Greeks, leaving just 3,000 survivors who were the only Persians to survive other than the 40,000 led by Artabazus.

The greatest courage in the battle was shown by the Persian foot soldiers and the cavalry of the Sacae, and personally by Mardonius himself. The Athenians and the Tegeans fought well, but the Lacedaemonians had fought and conquered the best troops. The bravest man on the day was Aristodemus, who was the only survivor from Thermopylae but he was denied any honours because, although he had fought bravely, he had sought out death, and so Posidonius, who had also fought bravely, but not coveted death, was thought a braver man. Callicrates, the most beautiful man of all of the Greeks, had been hit by an arrow and died, saying: 'I grieve not because I have to die for my country but because I have not lifted my arm against the enemy and been given the chance to die in glory'. Sophanes the Athenian also fought bravely, and it is said that he carried an iron anchor attached to his breastplate which he threw out before each attack so that he would not be able to retreat from his post.

The Mantineans arrived at this time to support the Greeks and were distressed to find the battle over, and imposed a fine on themselves and banished the commanders, as did the Elean force. The Mantineans wanted to pursue Artabazus, but Pausanias did not let them go. Pausanias was urged to crucify the body of Mardonius, as had been done to his uncle Leonidas, but Pausanias declined and ordered that the Helots should collect up all the spoils, for there were many tents adorned in silver and gold with many golden bowls and drinking cups. The Helots at this time stole many items which they sold to the Eginetans at a very low price. The spoils were divided up between the soldiers after a tenth had been set aside for the gods, and Pausanias received ten of every kind. The Plataeans found and concealed treasures of gold and silver for many years after the battle.

It is said that Pausanias had the Persian bakers and cooks prepare a meal in the tent of Mardonius which had been left with him by Xerxes and, at the same time, had his own cooks prepare a Spartan meal. He called the generals together and showed them the extravagant tent and the couches and tables with the fine banquet and served up both suppers as he observed: 'See the folly of the Persians when they enjoy fare such as this and come to rob us of our penury'.

The body of Mardonius disappeared the next day, and many have received large sums on this score from his son. The Lacedaemonians buried their dead in three graves, one for the youths and one for the Spartans and a third for the Helots. The Tegeans, Athenians, Megarians, and Phliasians also buried their dead, and even those nations that had arrived late for the battle built empty graves so that they might share in the glory for future generations.

The Greeks now held a council and resolved to make war on Thebes, at least until they gave up those men who had taken the side of the Medes, particularly their leaders, Timagenidas and Attaginus. The Greeks laid waste to the surrounding countryside and made attempts on the wall without ceasing for twenty days until Timagenidas addressed the Thebans: 'The Greeks are not likely to desist from their efforts until they take Thebes or you deliver us to them, so please find out whether they can be swayed by offering money from the treasury, for we were not alone in supporting the Persian King and if they do not take the money then you must offer us up to them'. The Thebans expected each man to be given a trial and the chance to escape with a bribe, so they offered them up, although Attaginus made his escape and his sons had to take his place. Pausanias spared the children, as he could not hold them accountable for the actions of their father, and Pausanias dismissed the Greek army and had the men offered up by the Thebans slain.

So it was that the Greek army won the land battle at Plataea and the army disbanded and returned to their homes.

DEPARTURE OF THE PERSIAN FLEET

Artabazus fled into Thessaly with his 40,000 men, claiming that Mardonius was just behind him so that he would not look weak and be attacked on the road. He used the shortest possible route but lost many men as they passed through Thrace, with many dying of fatigue and hunger, until eventually they reached Byzantium and crossed the strait into Asia.

The Persian fleet now consisted of three hundred ships, composed mostly of Medes and Persians, under the command of Mardontes, and had overwintered in Samos to make sure that the Ionians did not revolt while the

Greek fleet lay inactive at Delos under the command of Leotychides the Lacedaemonian.

On the same day as that of the battle of Plataea, three Samians came secretly from Samos, hiding their departure from the Persians and from the tyrant that the Persians had installed as ruler. The ambassadors related that: 'the Ionians need only see the Greek fleet arrive to take up arms and revolt from the Persians, who most likely would take flight'. Leotychides kept Hegesistratus, one of the ambassadors, with him, for he thought that his name would bring good fortune as he prepared the fleet for battle, while Deiphonus, the son of Evenius, prepared the sacrifices.

A strange thing happened to the father of the soothsayer, Evenius, who had fallen asleep one night in a cave while he guarded a flock of sheep which had been attacked by wolves, with sixty of the flock killed. Evenius was judged guilty of failing to keep watch and had his eyes put out, and from that time the sheep had no young and the land bore no harvest. The people sent to the Oracle and were told that they must give Evenius what he desired, for they had wrongfully deprived him of sight, as the gods themselves had sent the wolves. So the elders came to Evenius and offered him atonement for the wrong they had done him and wondered what he would like from them. Evenius had not heard of the word of the Oracle and asked for two of the best farms and a fine townhouse, which the elders paid for, after initially keeping the matter of the Oracle from him, much to his later indignation. Nevertheless, Evenius, at that moment, became a famous soothsayer.

The Greek fleet now sailed for Samos and set anchor at Calami, off the coast of Samos, near a temple of Hera, and prepared for battle. The Persians dismissed the Phoenicians and, not having the heart for battle, sailed for the mainland to the protection of the remainder of the land army stationed at Mycale to keep the Ionians under control. This army of sixty thousand men under the command of Tigranes dragged the ships ashore and built a rampart around them to protect both the ships and themselves from attack.

The Greeks sailed also to the mainland and prepared boarding bridges, and the like, and, when Leotychides saw the ramparts, he sailed up and down, exhorting the Ionians to revolt or fight meekly, repeating the strategy of Themistocles at Artemisium to bring the Ionians over to the Greek side or at least create some distrust between them and the Persians. The Greeks now disembarked and prepared for battle, while the Persians hastily disarmed the Samians and dispatched the Milesians to guard the heights of Mycale, so that they could be kept at a safe distance.

The Greeks heard a rumour that Mardonius had been defeated that very same day at Plataea and rushed forward with great purpose, for the Hellespont and the Islands were the prize of this battle. Both battles were fought on the same day of the same month, and the fighting took place near a sacred precinct of Eleusinian Demeter. The Athenians formed one half of the army and marched along the shore, while the Lacedaemonians marched across some hills to their destination, so by the time they arrived, the Athenians had already begun the battle.

The Persians put up a stout defence and even got the better of the battle, as long as their wicker bucklers stood, but once the Greeks burst through the line of shields, the Persians had to take refuge behind their ramparts. The Athenians, followed by the Corinthians, Sicyonians and Troezenians, pressed so closely that they followed them into the fortress and now only the Persian forces kept fighting, held together in knots of a few men, while the Greeks kept pouring in. The Persians lost two of their commanders but kept fighting until the Lacedaemonians joined in the remainder of the battle and many Greeks fell but the Persians were conquered. The Samians and other Ionians did everything they could to hinder the Persians, and the Milesians sent the fleeing Persians in the wrong direction and around in circles before they slew them, having seen the outcome of the battle.

The Athenians showed the greatest bravery in this battle and, when most of the Persians had been slain, they set fire to the ships and burnt the rampart, having first removed all the booty, which included caskets of money, to their ships. They then held a conference, for they thought it impossible to protect and guard Ionia, and the Persians were sure to want revenge. The Peloponnesians proposed that the populations of Ionia be given the cities of those Greeks who had taken sides with the Medes, but the Athenians preferred that the Ionians remain where they were and prevailed, so that the Samians, Chians, Lesbians and other islanders joined the league of Greek allies, binding themselves to be faithful and to share common cause with the Greeks.

The Persians who had survived took refuge in the heights of Mycale and marched toward Sardis, where Masistes, a son of Darius, reproached the commander, Artayntes, as being 'worse than a woman'. He became very angry and drew his scimitar and would have slain Masistes had he not been stopped by the guards.

XERXES IN SARDIS

Xerxes had spent all the time since he fled from Athens at Sardis and had fallen in love with the wife of his brother Masistes, against whom he could not use violence out of respect for his kin. His sister-in-law knew this and resisted his advances, so to further his desires, Xerxes arranged for his own son Darius to marry a daughter of this woman and Masistes. Xerxes arranged for the couple to be married and then departed for Susa and received the woman into the palace, whereupon his desires were now firmly placed in the direction of his new daughter-in-law, Artaynta, the daughter of Masistes, who soon returned his love.

Now Xerxes' own wife, Amestris, began to suspect and gave Xerxes a long robe of many colours which she had made herself and presented to her husband as a gift. Xerxes wore the robe and went to see Artaynta, who had pleased him greatly that day and he offered her anything she would like. She chose to ask for possession of the robe, whereupon Xerxes tried to get her to change her mind, offering her gold and whole cities, and even an army that would obey no other leader, to take in place of the robe. Artaynta now wore the robe and incited great anger in Amestris, who decided that Masistes' wife was to blame for the actions of her daughter. Consequently, on the day of the King's birthday, 'Tykta', as the feast is called in the Persian tongue, she asked for the wife of Masistes to be delivered into her power as the gift she could ask of the King. The King refused, but in the end, he had to yield but first tried to persuade Masistes to leave his wife, offering his own daughter as a new wife for him.

Masistes refused, and Xerxes grew angry 'What have you gained by refusing my daughter, for surely you shall no longer live with your wife. In time you must learn to accept what is offered to you and not cause offense by your refusal'. Masistes now withdrew saying only: 'Master, you have not taken my life'.

Masistes returned home to find that Amestris had ordered her guards to horribly mutilate and disfigure his wife and that she had been sent home with her ears cut off and her tongue cut out and thrown to the dogs. Masistes called his sons together and fled for Bactria, where he was satrap, and where he hoped to stir up revolt, but he was caught on the road and slain together with his own army. Such is the tale of the love of King Xerxes and the death of his brother Masistes.

Meanwhile, the Greek fleet sailed to the Hellespont, where they found the bridge at Abydos already destroyed, and they crossed over and laid siege to Sestos, although by now the Peloponnesians wanted to go home. The siege continued into late autumn, and now the Athenians also wanted to return home but were persuaded by their captains to stay. The town was guarded by both Persians and Aeolians, and with the walls almost breached and the food supplies exhausted, the Persians fled the city and the Aeolians opened the gates to the Greeks.

The whole district had been ruled by Artayctes, who had possessed himself of some sacred treasures and polluted the inner sanctuary of a temple by having intercourse there and had done other evil things and found himself totally unprepared for the Greeks' coming. A strange thing happened one day, when some salted fish began to leap and quiver as if they had only just been caught, and Artayctes saw this and said: 'Fear not because of this marvel, for it appears on my account for me to repay the riches I stole from the temple. I fix my fine at one hundred talents and will give a further two hundred talents if the Athenians spare me and my son'. However, he was not to be spared and was taken to the tongue of land where the bridges had been fixed and nailed to a board and made to watch as his son was stoned.

It was Artembares, the grandfather of this Artayctes, who had suggested to Cyrus in time gone by: 'O Cyrus, let us leave this poor land we dwell in and choose a country from the nations we have conquered with fairer land for us to live in, for which country with the power that we have would not choose to do so?' Cyrus did not like this counsel and said that they could move if they liked but 'prepare to be ruled by others, for soft countries gave birth to soft men and there was no region which produced both delightful fruits and warlike men', and so the Persians altered their view, acknowledging that Cyrus was right and better to live as Lords in a churlish land than to cultivate plains and be the slaves of others.

The Greek fleet now sailed back to Greece carrying many treasures, including the cables from the bridges, which they were to dedicate in their temples, and so the conflict between the Greeks and the Persians came to an end.

Index

Abdera 32
Abydos 107, 142
Adeimantus 135
Adrastus 10, 11
Agbatana 22, 30, 57
Alcanor 18
Alceus 5
Alexander 4, 143
Alyates 21
Alyattes 8, 16
Amasis 46, 54
Amazons 89
Ameinocles 120
Amestris 160
Amomphaterus 152
Anaxandides 14
Anaxaridias 75
Antipater 112
Apis 51, 57
Apollo 19
Apries 46
Arabia 67
Ardericca 33
Argives 9
Arianignes 138
Arion 6
Aristo 14
Aristophilides 72
Artabanos 104
Artabanus 105, 108, 134

Artabazanes 103
Artabazus 143, 153, 156
Artachares 112
Artaphernes 95, 99
Artayctes 161
Artembares 25
Artemesium 118
Artemisia 137
Artemisium 128, 158
Aspathines 58, 59
Assyria 23, 35
Assyrians 22
Astryages 20
Astyages 2, 11, 16, 24, 26, 28
Athena 13
Athenians 12, 14, 95, 99, 101, 103, 114, 133, 147, 152
Atistodemus 154
Atossa 58, 62, 71, 103
Attys 10
Axares 36, 37
Babylon 32, 35, 36
Babylonians 35, 76
Bagaeus 70
Boetia 145
Bosphorus 85
Callimachus 98

Cambyses 24, 46, 48, 49, 51, 55, 57, 64, 69
Candaules 1, 5
Capadocia 16
Caspian Sea 36
Cassandané 46
Chilon 12
Chios 31
Choaspes 34
Chromius 18
Cimon 96
Cleobis and Bito 9
Cleomenes 75
Croesus 8, 9, 10, 11, 12, 15, 16, 17, 18, 19, 30, 54
Cyaxares 16
Cyaxeres 16, 23, 24
Cyprus 36
Cyrus 2, 11, 16, 18, 19, 24, 26, 30, 32, 34, 36, 46, 64, 103
Darius 38, 58, 59, 61, 62, 64, 71, 73, 76, 77, 78, 85, 91, 93, 95, 99, 103, 125
Datis 95, 99
Deioces 22
Demeratus 103, 126
Democedes 71
Dionysius 43
Eginatan 138
Eginetan 119
Eginetans 115, 155
Egypt 49, 57

Egyptians . 40, 41, 46, 52
Epizelus 99
Eretria 95
Eretrians 96, 99
Erythraean sea 41
Erythraean Sea 84
Ethiopia 50
Europa 4
Eurybiades 128, 141, 143
Eurybiates 133, 134
Gelo 116
Gillus 73
Gobryas 58, 59, 92
Gorbryas 103
Greeks 41
Gyges 1, 5
Harpagus 17, 24, 26, 28, 31
Hecataeus 101
Helen 4
Helipolis 40
Hera 9
Heracleids 5
Hermonitimus 140
Hessiod 84
Hippias 97
Hippocrates 12
Histaeus 94
Homer 84
Hydarnes 58
Hyroedes 18
Hystapes 38, 58, 104
India 66
Intaphernes 58, 59, 75

Io 4
Ionians 30, 94, 158
Jardanus 5
Labynetus 34
Lacadaemonians 55, 144, 147, 151, 158
Lacedaemonians 12, 14, 18
Lake Maeotis 80, 85
Lake Meoris 40
Lake Moeris 64
Lemnos 101
Leonidas 122
Lichas 15
Lydia 4, 5
Madyes 23
Maeandrius 69, 74
Mandane 24
Mandrocles 85
Marathon 2, 96, 103
Mardonius 103, 139, 141, 143, 144, 150, 153, 155, 156, 158
Masistes 159
Massagetae 36
Mazares 31
Medea 4
Medes 12, 22, 23, 27, 29, 80, 122
Megabazus 94
Megabyzus 58, 60, 77
Megacles 13
Megacreon 112
Megistias 125
Memphis ... 48, 49, 51, 53
Miltiades 93, 96, 97, 99, 100, 101
Minos 69
Mitradates 24
Mneisiphilus 134
Nectoris 34
Nile 42, 48
Nineveh 23
Nitetis 46
Nitocris 33, 34
Oebares 62
Oeobazus 85
Olypipiodorus 147
Oroetes 69, 74
Otanes 58, 59, 60, 61, 74, 108
Othryadas 18
Pactyas 31
Panionius 140
Paros 99
Patiramphes 108
Pelasgians 101
Perdiccus 144
Periander 6
Persians 4, 18, 27, 28, 35, 90, 96, 114
Phalerum 135, 141
Phanes 47
Philippides 96
Phocians 124, 131, 143, 146, 149
Phoenicians 4
Phya 13
Pisistratus 12, 13, 96, 97
Plataeans 98

Polycrates 54, 69, 70, 71, 73
Posidonius 154
Prexaspes 53, 58, 59
Psammenitus. 47, 48, 49
Psammetichus 40, 42
Pteria 16
Pythius 106
Rhegium 32
River Ister 86
River Tigris 34
Salamis 134, 136
Samos 54, 73
Sandanis 15
Sardis 107
Scythian 36
Scythians 16, 23, 24, 28, 80, 82, 83, 85, 87, 89, 90, 93
Sicinnus 141
Siphnos 55
Smerdis 52, 57, 58
Solon 8, 10
Spargapises 38
Spartans 17, 30, 113

Susa 85, 99, 103, 109, 139
Syloson 73
Tegeans 14, 147, 153, 155
Telesarchus 74
Tellus 8
Thassos 112
Thebes 40
Themistocles 115, 134, 141, 143
Thermoplyae 118
Thermopylae 122, 130
Thracians 86
Thrasbylus 6
Tomyrius 2, 37
Velia 32
Xerxes 2, 103, 106, 109, 111, 112, 113, 114, 115, 120, 123, 126, 130, 134, 139, 142, 143, 159
Zeus 20
Zophyrus 77

www.ingramcontent.com/pod-product-compliance
Lightning Source LLC
Chambersburg PA
CBHW071925290426
44110CB00013B/1474